T0195583

THE LIVING ART

ART

A GUIDE TO LIFE, THE UNIVERSE AND EVERYTHING

ANAKAN ZILLIONAIRE "AZ"

BALBOA.
PRESS

A DIVISION OF HAY HOUSE

Copyright © 2018 Anakan Zillionaire "AZ".

All rights reserved. No part of this book may be used or reproduced by any means, graphic, electronic, or mechanical, including photocopying, recording, taping or by any information storage retrieval system without the written permission of the author except in the case of brief quotations embodied in critical articles and reviews.

Balboa Press books may be ordered through booksellers or by contacting:

Balboa Press
A Division of Hay House
1663 Liberty Drive
Bloomington, IN 47403
www.balboapress.com.au
1 (877) 407-4847

Because of the dynamic nature of the Internet, any web addresses or links contained in this book may have changed since publication and may no longer be valid. The views expressed in this work are solely those of the author and do not necessarily reflect the views of the publisher, and the publisher hereby disclaims any responsibility for them.

The author of this book does not dispense medical advice or prescribe the use of any technique as a form of treatment for physical, emotional, or medical problems without the advice of a physician, either directly or indirectly. The intent of the author is only to offer information of a general nature to help you in your quest for emotional and spiritual well-being. In the event you use any of the information in this book for yourself, which is your constitutional right, the author and the publisher assume no responsibility for your actions.

Any people depicted in stock imagery provided by Thinkstock are models, and such images are being used for illustrative purposes only. Certain stock imagery © Thinkstock.

Print information available on the last page.

ISBN: 978-1-5043-0973-8 (sc)
ISBN: 978-1-5043-0980-6 (e)

Balboa Press rev. date: 07/11/2018

THE LIVING ART

SEE YOUR DREAM REALITY
MADE MANIFEST IN EVERY MOMENT

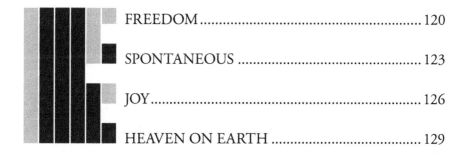

Dedication

Embrace
the bounty
of Universal
Magic

Even an Eclipse
of the full blue
moon comes along
every now &
again.

This book is dedicated
to you; for all the
dedication you've shown
in your own life.
May this book prove
itself useful to you.

Spirits thus exist and fly around by taking themselves and the world as lightly

Travel with lightness dear Universal One...

We move only in belief
Reality is solid, to those who
believe. For a new generation
of Dreamwalkers, & to onaid
keeping the Gateways &
Dreamtimes alive.

PREAMBLE

To the infinite one. Do you want your dream reality made manifest?!.
The book you have picked up is designed to aid you in attaining the
manifestation of your own individualised dream reality.

I hope you get as much inspiration from the content of this book as I did
within its creation.

When you are seeking some assistance open this book and look at it
periodically, then give this book the opportunity to help you in making
manifest the reality you so dream and wish to empower for yourself.

This book is a self-development / empowerment manual "a find, live and
be yourself book", designed as a tool and aid, enabling you to conducting
alignment of your dream reality.

The book covers all areas of life and reality in a fully embodied way, like
the Epicentre in the centre of the universe, enabling you to work through
the process of your current conditioned reality and to live in the creation
of the reality you truly desire in your life, always.

A basic method of engagement with this book is to have a thought, focus
or an essence towards or in relation to something. Look to the section
entitled "Suggested ways of engagement" section for further advice on
how one may choose to engage with this book, then choose a method of
engagement.

Read the imbuement of words, taking that which you will and discard that which doesn't serve you, or may not be felt to be of full resonance. What and who you are in this time, place and space. Trust in your intuitive self-guidance system, as life is a process, and all becomes ascended & built upon.

GUIDE

In opening this book I am dealing with what is. All is in harmony within whatever is going on, so remember to be at peace within the full dynamics of where, what and who you are.

An easy guide to life is to travel lightly and breathe as all is in harmony. I am ok, and as long as I make it to the end of the day I am doing fine.

Truth and purity will survive at the end of the day. I am who I am and that is me, so live it. Be honest and true, so if what is read does not fit or resonate as fullness for you pass on it, move on and take any of that which is befitting.

I am an individual & the infinite possibilities of me are insurmountable, incalculable and unparalleled to the infinite possibilities of another.

The life and living solution is worked within these pages, embrace ascension, carry yourself lightly and get all to fit with you in some manner, way, shape or form, this is to create the solid foundation of living in the solution - one rich in dynamic life giving energy.

It's a simple choice to walk the newer more life giving dream reality journey, just look at the here and now and apply the energy and movement required to see yourself in better stead in the future. Reapply the energy required to be your true full self.

Take what fits or you can easily learn from and leave the rest, as it may have pertinence in another time in another space, or for someone else.

Enjoy. Raison-de-etre, XOA.

HOW TO ENGAGE WITH THIS BOOK

The way this book has been designed is to toss a two sided object relating grey on one side of the object and black for the other.

Following the grey and black reference key on the side of each section or count and split the section in half every time you toss this will halve the overall probabilities every time one tosses. This must be done 10 times "5 times in the index & 5 times in the section you have been guided to".

Follow the grey and black reference key on the side of the index first. When the tossing procedure has been done in the index, refer to the pertinent section you have been guided to.

Then do the tossing procedure following the black and grey reference key in that section, this will refine the possibilities down to one answer, "your personal imbuement / answer (one answer out of the 1054 that this book has)".

This book helps one grow in conscious awareness and the aligning of oneself with your dream reality; thus aiding you in this journey called life.

This book may be seen as similar to a daily readings book, the tarot, the rune stones, or I-Ching, but is a mapmaker / for-tuning book. This book helps in the divining of answers with your individual will of self. This is done by co-relating placement, symbology or credence to the outcomes.

The easiest way of using this book is to leave it upside down with the words "Live the life you dream" showing.

Please do enjoy the process and journey of attaining your god-given birthright of having your dream reality, and this book in helping to bring it about into direct manifestation.

Broaden the scope of the questions or focus to create for a greater befittedness. This can be done by changing the focus / thought / essence, of the questions you are asking.

Read bigger blocks if required to end up with greater probabilities. This can be done by tossing less thus ending up with greater probabilities ie 2, 4, 8, 16, or a full section consisting of 32 probabilities, instead of one.

Take that which is most applicable or you can easily work with at any given point in time and space you might presently find yourself in. If you read through a full section, take only that which is of greatest resonance & is the most befitting, and do not take on or attach to that which does not fit for you.

Use discriminative wisdom "applied awareness", and where possible pick the best one to take with you; sometimes it's good 2 keep it simple. In simplifying less can a lot of the time be more, as it leads you to the fuller alignment of your energies. This will enaid you to being more of an essence will manifestor.

The section entitled "the map" may also prove valuable and has different ways in which 2 engage with this book.

To be what we individually are, enaids lightness, & the resolve required to breakthrough impasses. Enjoy, forge and live anew.

Lotza yumminess and wellwishing – Joie de vivre :-) AZ.

THE LIVING ART

Be at one with your life and know that you are all ready within your dream reality. Just for this to appear in your reality is a sure sign that you are where you are meant to be.

Read the commentary entitled "The Living Art" only if you are interested as it has reference to the book content, or feel free to move on to that which you will.

This book is designed to be processed each and every time one is with it. Give yourself all the time you require to process what is being offered in each and every moment.

You can find your self within this book. This book has 32 sections, with 32 sayings / passages in point form in each section "32 sections x 32 poinently formed passages = 1054 positively inspired imbuements", that pertain to the full dynamics of what life and reality, can be, at any given point in time.

It helps when empowered with tools and conscious awareness to enable, the creation of living life and reality the way you want it to be, whatever that is within the infinity of all that you are, can be and is yet to come.

The more you align the vessel of full self with this book, the greater the rewards will be. Live the imbuements like an aware, open honest living companion working in and with your life.

Emplace this book upside down when it's not in use & trust in your own inner guidance system as all is to be ascended and one needs to make one's own choices in life as this will aid your intuition & benefit you in creating your own picture and dream life for yourself.

The new ground is worked within these pages to create a solid foundation of self within the full richness that is all things, empowering you in this journey of life to attaining your dream reality.

The book will enaid you to get a degree in fully living life. This degree is all-encompassing, helping you to forge yourself into the future with strength and greater conscious awareness.

Once you know what you truly desire from your essence out, it lends to being a self-fulfilling prophecy, that is the alignment of all things.

Want for yourself that which others want for themselves, like peace of being, contentment, lightness, freedom, faith, security, wealth and the ability to be who and what you are anew.

Get all to resonate. Pull that which you desire into the world, and live it in and around you, where coincidence, synchronicity, de-ja-vu and providence will all become a natural part of the process within the unfolding.

What do you truly want as life. Now, when that is established, go about empowering it for yourself using discriminative wisdom and the power of positive attachment & look for the signals of it coming into your life.

Walk within the greater solution of living life, have enjoyment of the richness, diversity and process of all of that which life is.

The book may be seen as a self-development / empowerment manual, and acts as a protector and guardian in one's life.

The primary objective is to enable yourself to work through and process your current reality, and to guide you with tools to the achievement of being at one with your dream reality always.

Live within a practical application of spirituality, and your soul's journey, one that's simple and poignant for today's world. Forge, live and be the dream reality - whatever that may be within your full, unlimited, wish for self.

Determine and deem that which is food for thought and resonates as soul food. Apply the living art, and go about developing a fully embodying oneness with the synthesising universe.

Nurture the lateral beingness of living in the solution, while practicing discernment and discretion of that which you want / need / and is. Trust in your inner tuition which offers strength to your natural guidance system.

Apply an application of effort when entering into a conducive alignment of your full unfiltered self as inspiration is in the living.

Aid yourself to loosen the preoccupations in your life that inwardly are creating and outwardly manifesting dissonant vibrancy patterns, as these hinder the dream reality from manifesting.

Go about getting all to resonate and align your energy into an essence will manifestor of high potency. Create openings for positively inspired newness to come into the most suited spaces for your own development.

It's a self actuated process, aid your power; life is in the living and the best is yet to come, always. Allow the universe to help you as much as you go about helping yourself and have faith in the living force "that which wants that which you want for yourself" as you are entitled to a higher power & life of your own choosing.

Own your full self, as this helps create for a healthy, laterally imbued and infused holistic encompassment of that which is, can be and is yet to come.

Overall what this book brings is readaption and the realigning of your energies and beingness. Newer ways are used that are less held within the entrenchment of the limitations that one can directly draw upon oneself through the use of words, articulation / linguistics, conditioning and one's belief system.

Adapt to a new application and adaption within linguistics, and the use of articulation. This changes the perpetuation of outmoded ways of being and helps to bring greater richness forth when used in the present.

Words and letters, like numbers, have a discerning force and positioning of alignment. New wording and grammar is used to give a greater encapsulment of the fuller solution.

Every effort has been made in putting forth words in lighter, more life-giving ways such as "engaging", or "rich in dynamic life energies", instead of what the commonly held flip side might be.

This will help ascend the dualistic, and create for a paradigm shift, from the middle road to the divine sweet nectars of your own god nature.

The imbuings are going for greater resonance and purity within the englishly adapted human language of imaging, imparting a greater cohesive awareness of a fuller embroilment in the subtle arts, beingness and space creation.

When used and applied it brings into being, connectedness and cohesiveness with the nature of things. Thus greater encapsulment of positive alignment when delving into the poignant possibilities of this "find and live yourself book".

Move forth and determine that which is healthy input. Attach to the imbuings, dynamic values and latent lateral forces, as you will.

Shake yourself free, walk through the constrictions of the past and embrace that which is conducive and nurturing. Now, live your fuller self within the one, the all, and everything.

Aid yourself with the dream reality by already seeing manifest in this very divine moment of now. Your dream reality already exists, within the world you presently inhabit and within your consciousness build up. The / your full world of infinity, takes a paradigm and form of it's own; fully.

The power to make the world what you want is up to you. Watch for the signs. Give acknowledgment for having, holding, receiving, and the ability of creating within life and reality.

Live the magic and bestowings of the universe; now go forth and create being who you are anew - Follow your intuitive self into the expansion of your own individualised dream reality. Live the fuller more life-giving journey. Journey on. Dream reality.

This book is for the dynamic full beings of the universe (a generation of life artists). Go and appoint your way, sweet child of the universe.

SUGGESTED EXAMPLES
OF ENGAGEMENT

* <u>Anywhere and read map.</u>

* <u>Section map</u> – find the section of greatest pertaining value, go to that section and read through it, without stopping to analyse it, as it either fits or it doesn't, then pick the very best embuement / answer to take with you. Tis good to keep it simple, and just find the most fitting one, as it enaids becoming more clearly focused.

* <u>Answers Map</u> - Have a question / thought / focus / essence towards something "anything & of any nature", then use the tossing procedure to give you your answer.

* <u>In / Out Map</u> - Even in de-creating one is creating, as one is eternally creating. Something new in each and every moment, whether one is conscious of it or not.

* <u>Situation Map</u> – eg, guide yourself by asking questions in regards to life / relationships / money / love / actions, for the day or a situation etc.

* <u>For-tune Map</u> - Fortuning for the day / situation / an event, or it could be in regards to someone or with something etc. This enaids one's intuitive process and one's pre-cog abilities, and one's understanding of true nature.

*   <u>Empowerment Map</u> – Good for moving ahead, or knowing what is the best action to take. Use the force of your projected will, & full self. Come from purity of intention & motive as this will objectify life and reality by clearing away the debris and empowering the dream life for yourself, eg's – what should I do / how should I enact etc.

*   <u>Create your own map</u> – create a map / picture of engagement if so desired as this book is strong in versatile adaptability and has a strong essence of working in ways that are conducive to who & what we individually are.

*   <u>Anything map</u> – ie giving credence, symbology or an imbuement towards a reference point, like using a preordained map, that one could find in a tarot deck / a rune book / the i-ching or elsewhere. One may do this by briefing and using any other reference point and associating it / them to this book.

*   <u>Group and interpersonal map</u> – Offering an interpretation (first start with the person in focus); commenting. Rounds – final round – the players, in turn, offer what new insights have come to them concerning the commentary on the relative insights. Take turns, get along, communicate, listen, learn, readapt... Clarity & solidness be with you.

The art of objectification "to give placement, creadance ie – to hold in view, form or to put a solid embodiment around or with". Visionary channelling & mediumship. This book has a strong essence of working in ways that are conducive to who and what we individually are, physically, mentally and spiritually (P.M.S.).

*   3 Part Resolve Map – Challenge => Middle Ground
    => Solution "pick one or more for each"

    Challenge – Resolve that which there is strong mutables around as this
    will help clear & present the way.

    There may be a rich dynamic play presently that may be taking of
    your energy and or focal strengths, help yourself to bring about the
    solution you require.

    Create & enaid greater light to be shone into the situation by touching
    in on what it is and clarifying the pertinent issue that requires
    addressing.

    Address by touching / feeling in on that which does not resonate or
    requires resonance around. This helps to create fuller atonement this
    is done by discerning what it is, or where the energy is rooted and is
    coming from.

    It may involve finding the conscious awareness of what is in play.
    Addressing the shadows of that which may still have some credence
    or holding factor in your life at this point in time.

    It may be, you are looking into a gorge and you need to get to the other
    side which may seem presently impossible, simply click your mindset
    differently like – get the tools, build a bridge and get over it, jump in
    that spaceshuttler that is your vechile and individualised self and cruise
    the waves; ascend to a higher more life-giving way of being.

    Middle ground / the centre / core – Keep faith, things are working
    out and one is where one is meant to be and find that where you are
    now is enaiding you into your dream reality, whether you are presently
    aware of it or not.

    Live in & work towards the solution, like I am who I am and it is
    what it is.

Relax – use discerned wisdom "your own intuitive compass" and be aware of that which you allow in as input, and empower.

See divinely made manifest, ascending beyond your present best envisioning for yourself.

Going beyond that which you may have seen or previously envisaged as your reality or for yourself "give thanks for getting to this point in now land – well done".

Solution – Taking that which fits or that which one can easily apply and use and leave the rest for another time in another space.

Look for & live within the positive resolve mechanism & solution. One is eternally creating, create something new, fresh and inspirational.

Live & find manifest your own individual conception of the Big Picture. The infinite prossibilities of you are insurmountable, & incalculable to the infinite possibilities of another, one is entitled to a dream reality of one's own choosing.

Live within the manifestation of your dream reality, as it is already there living its own existence in full form in a world parallel and not 2 distant from the world you presently find yourself aboding.

THE WHOLEY 3 MAP / THE WHOLEY TRINITY

"Self, all, one (3 fold map / cosync)"

Universal / 0; "The biggest picture" – The full dance of self. The divine oneness of all that is, can be and is yet to come.

Anything perceivable is possible. The one, the all, and everything. Best outcome or new situation. If it is envisaged, it already exists within the world of infinite possibilities.

My Universe has a centre that is everywhere and a circumference that is nowhere, it is no-thing, yet it is everything.

Infinite multi-galactic interstellar utopian inter-paradigm multi-dimentional universal spacesurfing of divine individualised appointing.

A flap of a butterfly's wings is felt on the other side of the universe. Divine union. Infinity times infinity is infinity. Infinity and beyond.

Subjective => Objective => Receptive – / +; "Situation / You" - one was born into one's natural and god-given immaculate conception birthright of L.U.E. "Life, the Universe, & Everything", it is then a process of walking and living within the resolvable impasse required 2 live within your dream reality, always; ie – a conscious conducive alignment of your own individual reality.

The instrument of self and will around the mutable lore of all that is, that one sets up and attaches to as reality from the programming level.

It is a process of working through your conditioning, beliefs, and one's built up construct of self around what one believes to be so.

The realigning & greater aligning of one's focused intention. It is always positive; even in elimination & subtracting one is positively creating and moving forward with right action.

Relative - Challenge or action. The prevailing winds, the build up of tangibly held conscious reality.

What lies between heaven and earth? That which lies between the etheric and the most densified of the conditioned universe.

The relative build up of Life, the Universe and Everything "L.U.E.". Based around – Time, matter, light, gravity, levity, magnetism, etc.

Physically, Mentally, and Spiritually "P.M.S. of life and reality". Mind, Body, Soul, Spirit.

The built up play and dance of it all.

TIME WHEEL MAP

O – Centre / The Core "Self" - That which connects everything. The whole picture / is'ness together. The all encompasser.

! - Present – That which is of strongest influence or pertinence in your life at the moment.

X – Past – That which is waning in influence in your life, where you've come from or what you've just come through.

+ - Future – That which is coming into your life and is going to be of strongest influence in the future.

= - Underlining – That which is hidden, below, not so apparent, or clearly seen, or may just require conscious recognition.

This is a find, live and be yourself book. Be here now and remember that truth, purity, love and a clearer understanding with the nature of things survive all obstacles at the end of the day. Now – What would you like to see in your own life inwardly and outwardly?.

THE MAP

* I leave you hoping that the flame of liberation will burn in your heart, that "no shadow of a doubt" all are created free and equal that you too can have the reality you desire.

* Just hearing that you can manifest your own reality is a sure sign that you are on your way to achieving that which you desire in your life.

* This is a map or working guide, work from it, take that which fits and leave the rest, for another time in another space.

* Have you ever had a question you needed to know the answer to?. Go from looking to finding, having & beholding. Have manifest in each and every moment the resolvable impasse you require.

* Have you ever known what it's like to know full freedom and lightness?. Re-kindle the seeds of that which you most desire.

* Do you wish and deeply desire .... to come true?, Has any of it been bestowed. Think of all the good times, look to the positive and that which advocates such.

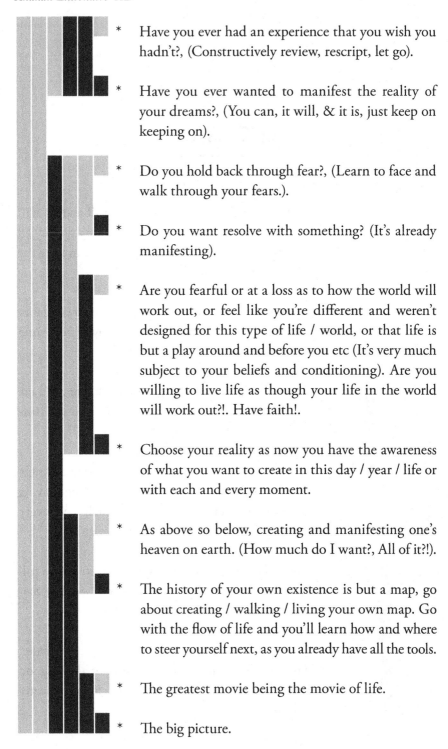

* Have you ever had an experience that you wish you hadn't?, (Constructively review, rescript, let go).

* Have you ever wanted to manifest the reality of your dreams?, (You can, it will, & it is, just keep on keeping on).

* Do you hold back through fear?, (Learn to face and walk through your fears.).

* Do you want resolve with something? (It's already manifesting).

* Are you fearful or at a loss as to how the world will work out, or feel like you're different and weren't designed for this type of life / world, or that life is but a play around and before you etc (It's very much subject to your beliefs and conditioning). Are you willing to live life as though your life in the world will work out?!. Have faith!.

* Choose your reality as now you have the awareness of what you want to create in this day / year / life or with each and every moment.

* As above so below, creating and manifesting one's heaven on earth. (How much do I want?, All of it?!).

* The history of your own existence is but a map, go about creating / walking / living your own map. Go with the flow of life and you'll learn how and where to steer yourself next, as you already have all the tools.

* The greatest movie being the movie of life.

* The big picture.

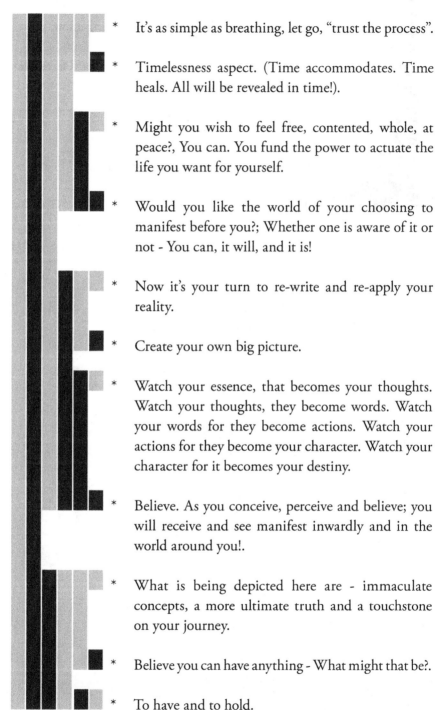

* It's as simple as breathing, let go, "trust the process".

* Timelessness aspect. (Time accommodates. Time heals. All will be revealed in time!).

* Might you wish to feel free, contented, whole, at peace?, You can. You fund the power to actuate the life you want for yourself.

* Would you like the world of your choosing to manifest before you?; Whether one is aware of it or not - You can, it will, and it is!

* Now it's your turn to re-write and re-apply your reality.

* Create your own big picture.

* Watch your essence, that becomes your thoughts. Watch your thoughts, they become words. Watch your words for they become actions. Watch your actions for they become your character. Watch your character for it becomes your destiny.

* Believe. As you conceive, perceive and believe; you will receive and see manifest inwardly and in the world around you!.

* What is being depicted here are - immaculate concepts, a more ultimate truth and a touchstone on your journey.

* Believe you can have anything - What might that be?.

* To have and to hold.

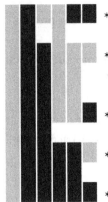

* Live the life you imagined, reinventing anew.

* Living and walking your dreams can have the broadest of dreams come true.

* To live your immaculate dream.

* Having it all, in all ways and on all levels.

* Total resolution.

REFLECTIVE SELF
(Me / You "Oneself")

* Taking that which fits and throwing the rest over your shoulder.

* Reflective. Like having a two way mirror where you are protected from external influences while having the objectivity of seeing yourself.

* May the answers come to you freely and easily, or the questions to find the answers, so as to feel one has depicted (in the fullest sense) that which one desires...

* The heart of the wise, "like a mirror", should reflect all objects without being sullied by anything.

* The looking glass. I am who I am and that is me.

* Things lose their power when one no longer attaches to whatever it is that one gives one's power to.

* Better constructs - beauty exudes, good / great things happen, beautiful experiences and exchanges abound, the world is working out. The world of my deepest desire is manifesting before me moment by moment.

* Be aware of the power of attachment to one's belief system "ascending outmoded constructs".

* Attach to that which one wishes to have manifest inwardly, or to be surrounded by in one's life.

* Budda under the bhodi tree "what is it one desires", it can be a better construct than anything pre-imagined, he got what he essentially wanted; it's all but a map, what map does one wish to create for oneself. Re-member infinity times infinity is still infinity.

* How does one percieve that everything is but a reflection?, One can go as far as to dip within the void and create one's own universe, or one can take it to the other extreme where everything is but love, light and every possible linkage is obtained, or one may like to watch a symbiotic collection of your conditioning before you. What is it one truly wants?; maybe start by putting forth knowledge of what you would like.

* Disonance, for example things change – Planetary, Non-pollution, Self sufficiency, Energy industry, Education, Health, Re-forestation, the powers that be, ones relationship to oneself or the world in which one finds oneself, etc?. How does it fit in the world within, as that is what has the outside repercussions whether one is consciously aware of it or not. Is one growing in conscious awareness of the repercussions of one's omnipresence / omnipotential?, (Be careful of what one empowers or attaches to, as one is eternally creating!).

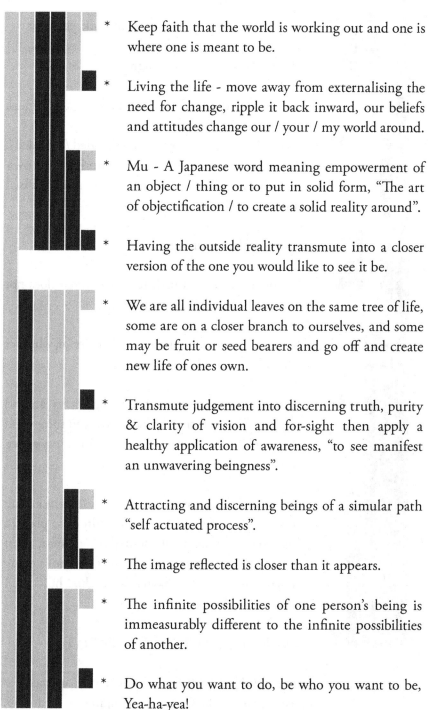

* Keep faith that the world is working out and one is where one is meant to be.

* Living the life - move away from externalising the need for change, ripple it back inward, our beliefs and attitudes change our / your / my world around.

* Mu - A Japanese word meaning empowerment of an object / thing or to put in solid form, "The art of objectification / to create a solid reality around".

* Having the outside reality transmute into a closer version of the one you would like to see it be.

* We are all individual leaves on the same tree of life, some are on a closer branch to ourselves, and some may be fruit or seed bearers and go off and create new life of ones own.

* Transmute judgement into discerning truth, purity & clarity of vision and for-sight then apply a healthy application of awareness, "to see manifest an unwavering beingness".

* Attracting and discerning beings of a simular path "self actuated process".

* The image reflected is closer than it appears.

* The infinite possibilities of one person's being is immeasurably different to the infinite possibilities of another.

* Do what you want to do, be who you want to be, Yea-ha-yea!

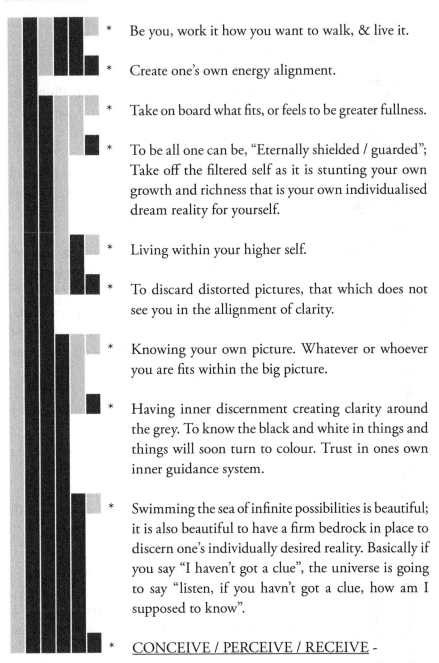

* Be you, work it how you want to walk, & live it.

* Create one's own energy alignment.

* Take on board what fits, or feels to be greater fullness.

* To be all one can be, "Eternally shielded / guarded"; Take off the filtered self as it is stunting your own growth and richness that is your own individualised dream reality for yourself.

* Living within your higher self.

* To discard distorted pictures, that which does not see you in the allignment of clarity.

* Knowing your own picture. Whatever or whoever you are fits within the big picture.

* Having inner discernment creating clarity around the grey. To know the black and white in things and things will soon turn to colour. Trust in ones own inner guidance system.

* Swimming the sea of infinite possibilities is beautiful; it is also beautiful to have a firm bedrock in place to discern one's individually desired reality. Basically if you say "I haven't got a clue", the universe is going to say "listen, if you havn't got a clue, how am I supposed to know".

* CONCEIVE / PERCEIVE / RECEIVE -

The CONCEPTION of conceive / perceive / receive would be: Conceive "conjure up, dream up, form, initiate, plan, invent"; Perceive "affirmation, empowerment of, opening up to, catch sight of, discern, detect, discover, distinguish, recognise"; Receive "be given, accept into one's life, come by, come into, get, obtain, to experience, let in, meet, greet, welcome, have bestowed".

The <u>PERCEPTION</u> of conceive / perceive / receive would be: One has the power to ascend anything (discard and or leave behind) and create anything ⁓ One has the potential of the omnipotent god creator within ⁓ One has the power to create one's heaven on earth and a universe of ones choosing ⁓ One is where one is meant to be.

The <u>RECEPTION</u> of conceive / perceive / receive would be: To possess, ⁓ To dream up and have actualise, ⁓ To feel, be & live the embodiment of whatever it is, very solidly in ones life. I am a god creator and have the power to manifest the reality and a universe of my choosing, whatever that may happen to be.

INNER KNOWING

* Live one's own version of reality.

* One's deepest essence.

* Open all the doors and keep them open. Develop a knowledge of where one stands so one can come from a more pure driven omnipotent nature.

* Own one's shadow (that which causes fluctuances, or one to shudder, inwardly detox / trip, that which brings dis-ease or doesn't feel / sit right, as it's all O.K. you will soon learn the lateral abilities of walking within your fuller freer self. Through conscious awareness and knowing where one stands in things, the resolve and bridging work comes to replace the outmoded parts of self. They will die away and the breath of fresh air that is life will be bestowed. Give thanks and pat yourself on the back as you are doing mighty fine.

* It is what it is, you are who you are. Live your own fullest being "deepest belief system", & then nurture it till you see it made manifest". Rather than have one foot on the brake, and one foot on the accelerator, take your foot off the brake, you're going to be looked after as your in-tuition and self-actuated guidance system will take hold to help guide your

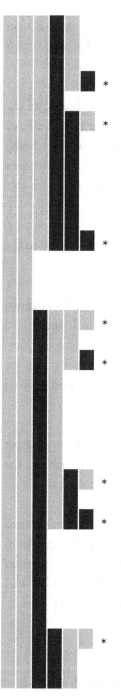

light of your infinite spirit self. You will soon learn how and where to first apply and steer yourself.

* O.K. It's all ok, O.K?!; O.K.

* Within a trip there isn't a trip, as one never loses self; Have faith, be open to the resolve and that which may bring about centredness and provodential deliverance in one's wishes, desires and energy, thus one will find it made manifest.

* What peace and joy there is in being. Even the most macabre depictionisms may hide or have prothetic beauty.

* Connectedness / Interconnection (Interrelatedness).

* Reflective self. Knowing where one is within things or to know where one isn't, lending oneself energetically away from that which is not doing it for one, and into the conduction of that which is. Self assured and realised.

* I, In, Inner knowing.

* Within and without (A lateral beingness). Gain composure with such as it's one of the most omnipotent ways of being in manifesting and realising one's inner potential and greater dream reality.

* Perception, conception?, "looking at one's conditioning and how that materialises in one's inner and outer life".

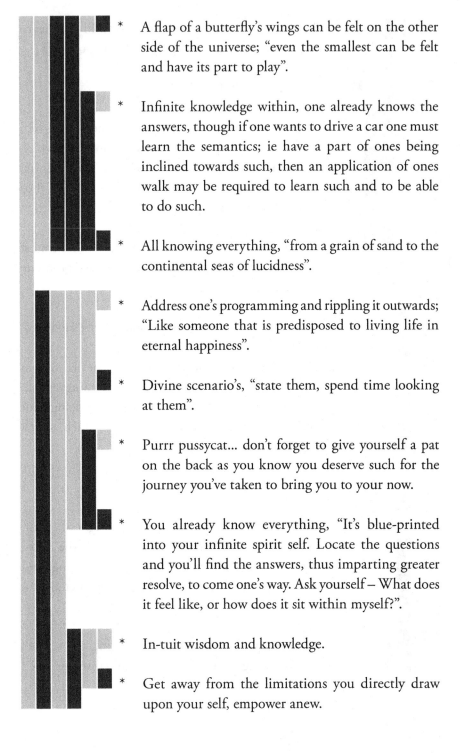

* A flap of a butterfly's wings can be felt on the other side of the universe; "even the smallest can be felt and have its part to play".

* Infinite knowledge within, one already knows the answers, though if one wants to drive a car one must learn the semantics; ie have a part of ones being inclined towards such, then an application of ones walk may be required to learn such and to be able to do such.

* All knowing everything, "from a grain of sand to the continental seas of lucidness".

* Address one's programming and rippling it outwards; "Like someone that is predisposed to living life in eternal happiness".

* Divine scenario's, "state them, spend time looking at them".

* Purrr pussycat... don't forget to give yourself a pat on the back as you know you deserve such for the journey you've taken to bring you to your now.

* You already know everything, "It's blue-printed into your infinite spirit self. Locate the questions and you'll find the answers, thus imparting greater resolve, to come one's way. Ask yourself – What does it feel like, or how does it sit within myself?".

* In-tuit wisdom and knowledge.

* Get away from the limitations you directly draw upon your self, empower anew.

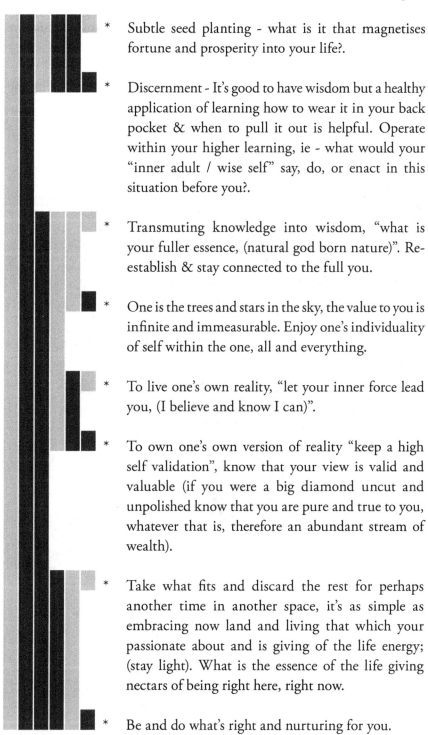

* Subtle seed planting - what is it that magnetises fortune and prosperity into your life?.

* Discernment - It's good to have wisdom but a healthy application of learning how to wear it in your back pocket & when to pull it out is helpful. Operate within your higher learning, ie - what would your "inner adult / wise self" say, do, or enact in this situation before you?.

* Transmuting knowledge into wisdom, "what is your fuller essence, (natural god born nature)". Re-establish & stay connected to the full you.

* One is the trees and stars in the sky, the value to you is infinite and immeasurable. Enjoy one's individuality of self within the one, all and everything.

* To live one's own reality, "let your inner force lead you, (I believe and know I can)".

* To own one's own version of reality "keep a high self validation", know that your view is valid and valuable (if you were a big diamond uncut and unpolished know that you are pure and true to you, whatever that is, therefore an abundant stream of wealth).

* Take what fits and discard the rest for perhaps another time in another space, it's as simple as embracing now land and living that which your passionate about and is giving of the life energy; (stay light). What is the essence of the life giving nectars of being right here, right now.

* Be and do what's right and nurturing for you.

* Time for a shift ~ new directions "transmute and live your own big picture".

* Operate within embracing your own true reality and essence of self.

FAITH

* A seed of faith ~ as strong as everything, and as transparent as an unformed light particle; Imagine it a very strong seed / tree, keep on watering, nurturing and composting the seed, it will grow ending up being big & strong with offspring of its own.

* Once the seed of liberation takes root it is a plant of rapid growth; The universe wishes to lead you where you wish to lead yourself, dream a little dream for yourself.

* Facets of faith being hope, trust and prair "PRAIR being - PRA, prana within the AIR, aether (spirit substance)", the smallest is felt like a flap of a butterfly's wings being felt on the other side of the universe.

* Do not to attach to doubt, instil positive reinforcement.

* Faith that things are going as they should.

* Essence - what peace there is in being "letting go being light, free & at ease Create for the sort of person to trip over a bar of gold as he is taking life as it comes and in his stride)".

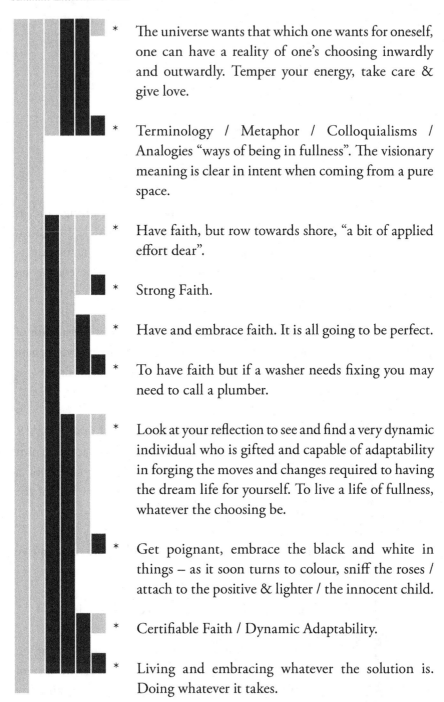

* The universe wants that which one wants for oneself, one can have a reality of one's choosing inwardly and outwardly. Temper your energy, take care & give love.

* Terminology / Metaphor / Colloquialisms / Analogies "ways of being in fullness". The visionary meaning is clear in intent when coming from a pure space.

* Have faith, but row towards shore, "a bit of applied effort dear".

* Strong Faith.

* Have and embrace faith. It is all going to be perfect.

* To have faith but if a washer needs fixing you may need to call a plumber.

* Look at your reflection to see and find a very dynamic individual who is gifted and capable of adaptability in forging the moves and changes required to having the dream life for yourself. To live a life of fullness, whatever the choosing be.

* Get poignant, embrace the black and white in things — as it soon turns to colour, sniff the roses / attach to the positive & lighter / the innocent child.

* Certifiable Faith / Dynamic Adaptability.

* Living and embracing whatever the solution is. Doing whatever it takes.

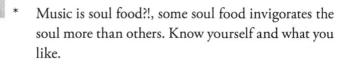

* Music is soul food?!, some soul food invigorates the soul more than others. Know yourself and what you like.

* Be happy, light and free!. Are you feeling lightness within the lingering taste of now?!.

* BEING ~ Stress less, Be more!, and enjoy extasy.

* You are unchallenged, you just work within a framework of a typically held belief of reality, the typical belief is challenged elsewhere!. A new emergence of all sorts of beliefs / dreamtimes and realities are within the world you inhabit. Some are more cohesive and reflective of your own, and all conducive and indicative of a world of possibilities and the embrace of a fully embodied alignment.

* Be what you desire inwardly and outwardly.

* It is perfectly fine to have dreams and aspirations; let it be divinity, and providence made manifest in the journey, to have such things turn into solidification. Look for the signs in your day to day life, and in the sweetest nectars of now that validates such.

* Everything is going to plan - just readapt your current situation with the tools you've got. The tools can be people, places, ways of being, anything.

* Final liberation, freedom and oneness. The essence of one's journey is fully in sync. You are a clear pure vessel of who you are and what you want to be and become always. Some ways of being or living fullness create and see manifest easier.

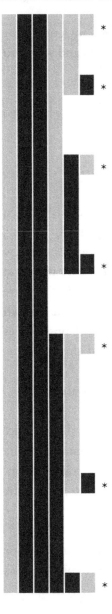

* Your life has brought you to where you are, have faith!

* Slow down. Make an assets list of all you have inwardly; put focus on the good & empowering, go forth and conquer.

* Universe walk with me, support me on my journey, conquer and show me the path with whatever I may choose to do, or wherever I might decide to steer myself.

* Certifiable Faith. It will all work out, your fine and everything is going to groove just perfectly so travel light dear universally spirited one.

* One is never moving backwards on one's journey. Have faith, learn to steer yourself. Work towards the solution with small steps of moving forward. Stay in the solution as that creates for giant leaps in your life. Each step generates momentum, and greater allignment.

* Resolve comes to those who play the game of life as holistically as possible while having both feet fully embedded on firm ground, "whatever that firm ground may be".

* The universe helps those that help themselves. Create an inner space of being it, then outwardly live and have it.

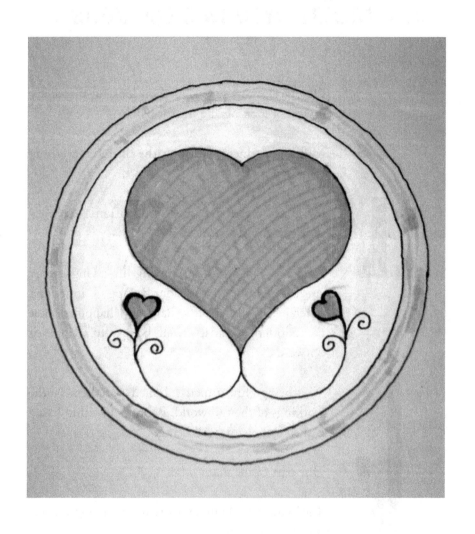

THE MULTI-DYNAMIC UNIVERSE

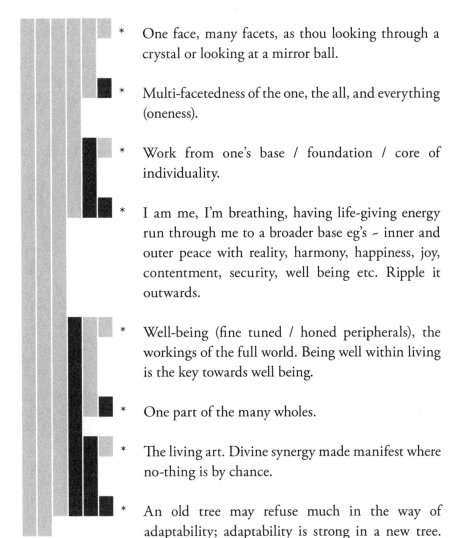

* One face, many facets, as thou looking through a crystal or looking at a mirror ball.

* Multi-facetedness of the one, the all, and everything (oneness).

* Work from one's base / foundation / core of individuality.

* I am me, I'm breathing, having life-giving energy run through me to a broader base eg's ~ inner and outer peace with reality, harmony, happiness, joy, contentment, security, well being etc. Ripple it outwards.

* Well-being (fine tuned / honed peripherals), the workings of the full world. Being well within living is the key towards well being.

* One part of the many wholes.

* The living art. Divine synergy made manifest where no-thing is by chance.

* An old tree may refuse much in the way of adaptability; adaptability is strong in a new tree.

Adapt & grow a new tree for yourself from the leaves of knowledge, and the seeds of now.

* The complexities of things are usually quite smooth and simple and once one knows and learns what they are.

* The best way to learn is to experience, give living your life the way you want. Wondering why things are placed where they are can be extraneous. Try immersing yourself into life without the need to evaluate or understand. Let the self-actuated guidance system & your higher in-tuition take hold.

* Stay light within your dreams, aspirations and daily living. Walk forwards unfettered. Your map and infinite possibilities are unfathomable compared to the possibilities of another. Put focus and footwork into you own journey.

* Work within the dynamics and full embroilment of is'ness, and by gaining an understanding and foothold within that which you require greater understanding, knowledge and awareness as it may find itself still in play. Pertinance in life and to that of your future life and living.

* Learn to steer yourself based on what you know.

* Life's here to be enjoyed and has many attributes, one can always say life is rich and dynamic in whatever that pertains to in your current reality.

* What do you enjoy in your current reality?. What have you enjoyed in the past?.

* Oneness.

* Life in the fast lane, life in the slow lane, life with no lanes and life in a traffic jam, & life on a country lane - are all in harmony and sync. Whatever state one is in, one is in sync (own the full gamut of your being and things will find harmony and flow).

* Enjoy life in all its eccentricities.

* Jump in that shuttle and cruise the waves, ascend to a higher more life-giving way of being.

* Pace your energy - use constructive applied effort & know when to steer your energies in a more conducive manner; "that which will create for greater alignment".

* Live life to its fullest.

* Be who you are within the big picture of your own individualised synthesising universe.

* Let go. It is what it is and you are what you are. If it's meant to be it will be; one can only do so much before working in aversion to the process; steering your energies elsewhere and being within that which is beneficial".

* It is what it is; Live it, be it, do it.

* Is, what is, is; learn to transmute objects of design and receive things in a new way so as to be of a greater life giving energy to you.

* It may prove to be very benificial to take the full you with you and not blink or squint into / onto life. Bring your full beingness to the party, and have some excellent fun.

* Small is good, very good sometimes.

* Chew it up, consume, compost. Live & ascend the old & embrace the new. Enjoy a richer base for growth.

* This is exactly what the conscious need.

* The sands of time "constructively review the past, then positively flaunt it into the future".

* Apparatus operatus "get into the solution".

* LIFE - the game play in action. Reality is solid to those that believe in all things while being within a life and paradyme of one's own reckoning.

CENTRE

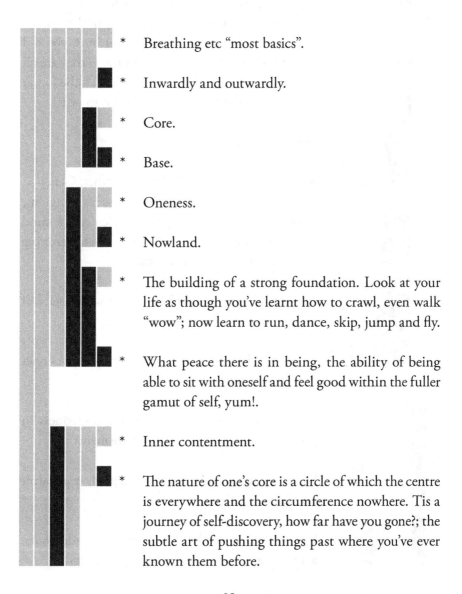

* Breathing etc "most basics".

* Inwardly and outwardly.

* Core.

* Base.

* Oneness.

* Nowland.

* The building of a strong foundation. Look at your life as though you've learnt how to crawl, even walk "wow"; now learn to run, dance, skip, jump and fly.

* What peace there is in being, the ability of being able to sit with oneself and feel good within the fuller gamut of self, yum!.

* Inner contentment.

* The nature of one's core is a circle of which the centre is everywhere and the circumference nowhere. Tis a journey of self-discovery, how far have you gone?; the subtle art of pushing things past where you've ever known them before.

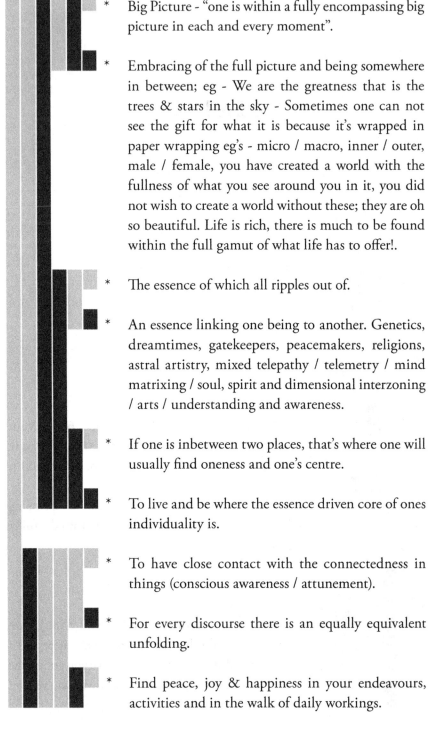

* Big Picture - "one is within a fully encompassing big picture in each and every moment".

* Embracing of the full picture and being somewhere in between; eg - We are the greatness that is the trees & stars in the sky - Sometimes one can not see the gift for what it is because it's wrapped in paper wrapping eg's - micro / macro, inner / outer, male / female, you have created a world with the fullness of what you see around you in it, you did not wish to create a world without these; they are oh so beautiful. Life is rich, there is much to be found within the full gamut of what life has to offer!.

* The essence of which all ripples out of.

* An essence linking one being to another. Genetics, dreamtimes, gatekeepers, peacemakers, religions, astral artistry, mixed telepathy / telemetry / mind matrixing / soul, spirit and dimensional interzoning / arts / understanding and awareness.

* If one is inbetween two places, that's where one will usually find oneness and one's centre.

* To live and be where the essence driven core of ones individuality is.

* To have close contact with the connectedness in things (conscious awareness / attunement).

* For every discourse there is an equally equivalent unfolding.

* Find peace, joy & happiness in your endeavours, activities and in the walk of daily workings.

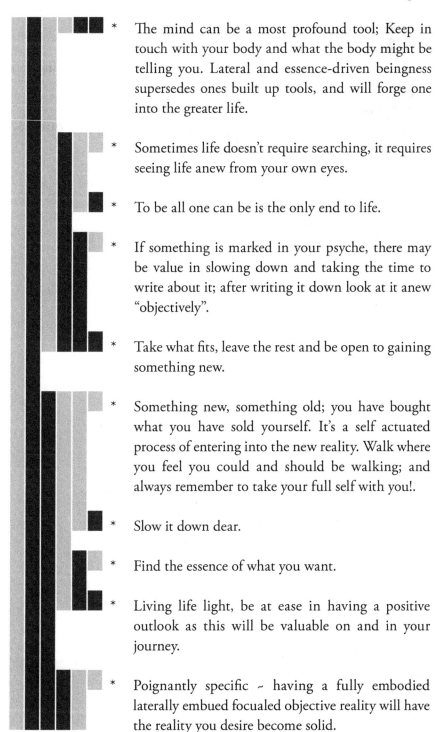

* The mind can be a most profound tool; Keep in touch with your body and what the body might be telling you. Lateral and essence-driven beingness supersedes ones built up tools, and will forge one into the greater life.

* Sometimes life doesn't require searching, it requires seeing life anew from your own eyes.

* To be all one can be is the only end to life.

* If something is marked in your psyche, there may be value in slowing down and taking the time to write about it; after writing it down look at it anew "objectively".

* Take what fits, leave the rest and be open to gaining something new.

* Something new, something old; you have bought what you have sold yourself. It's a self actuated process of entering into the new reality. Walk where you feel you could and should be walking; and always remember to take your full self with you!.

* Slow it down dear.

* Find the essence of what you want.

* Living life light, be at ease in having a positive outlook as this will be valuable on and in your journey.

* Poignantly specific ~ having a fully embodied laterally embued focualed objective reality will have the reality you desire become solid.

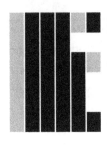

* Discern and embrace the new.

* Lighten up as the universe is here supporting you as a being.

* Lighten up, eg the reason fairies can fly is that they take life and the world so lightly.

DILIGENCE

* Keep on keeping on.

* Taking of the energy ~ take of the energy and transmute the objects of design into a positive force.

* Keep it simple. A journey of a million kilometers begins with one step. Q - How does an ant eat an elephant? A - One bite at a time. Double A - Most of life is in the enjoyment of the process.

* Baby steps. How much can I do in one day?.

* Finishing projects, "I will to will thy will".

* Goal setting, start with the small, and go about accomplishing the big.

* Steering ones energy best.

* Work on that which is in front of one.

* The universe helps and accommodates those that help themselves.

* Nurture that which is of benefit.

* Employing one's time most constructively.

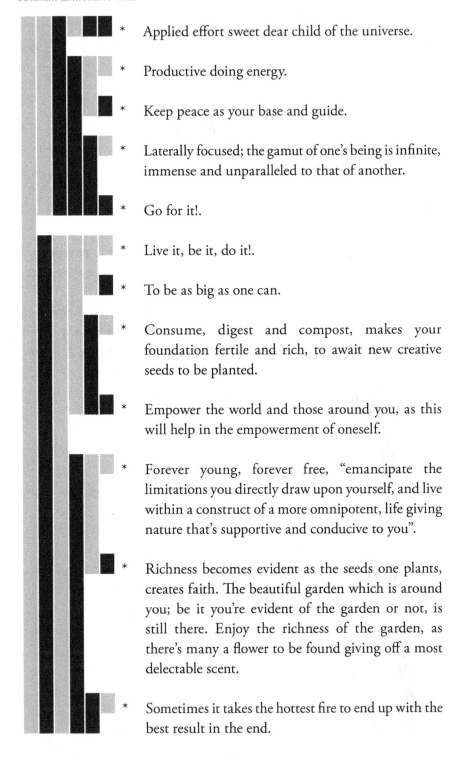

* Applied effort sweet dear child of the universe.

* Productive doing energy.

* Keep peace as your base and guide.

* Laterally focused; the gamut of one's being is infinite, immense and unparalleled to that of another.

* Go for it!.

* Live it, be it, do it!.

* To be as big as one can.

* Consume, digest and compost, makes your foundation fertile and rich, to await new creative seeds to be planted.

* Empower the world and those around you, as this will help in the empowerment of oneself.

* Forever young, forever free, "emancipate the limitations you directly draw upon yourself, and live within a construct of a more omnipotent, life giving nature that's supportive and conducive to you".

* Richness becomes evident as the seeds one plants, creates faith. The beautiful garden which is around you; be it you're evident of the garden or not, is still there. Enjoy the richness of the garden, as there's many a flower to be found giving off a most delectable scent.

* Sometimes it takes the hottest fire to end up with the best result in the end.

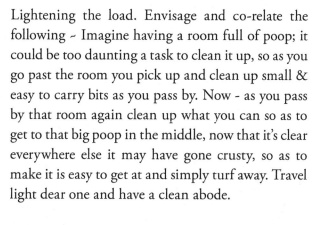

* Lightening the load. Envisage and co-relate the following ~ Imagine having a room full of poop; it could be too daunting a task to clean it up, so as you go past the room you pick up and clean up small & easy to carry bits as you pass by. Now - as you pass by that room again clean up what you can so as to get to that big poop in the middle, now that it's clear everywhere else it may have gone crusty, so as to make it is easy to get at and simply turf away. Travel light dear one and have a clean abode.

* Forge yourself a-head.

* There is no time like the present, the present is a gift in whatever form it comes, learn to readapt the present in such a way that it is a gift. Life is rich.

* Make yourself do it.

* Live life to the fullest, life is too precious to be holding back.

* Does the smaller voice have something to say? Listen to and empower your fuller being.

* Get out of your life that which no longer fits.

* Simple prairs for the soul's journey can work as a valuable asset; ie may resolve come, and the reality I so desire manifest.

* If you want to know your past look at your present condition, if you want to know your future look at your current action.

MEMORY

* The ability to be able to recapture, recollect, recall, review, remember...

* Retrieval - The ability to be able to recall with ease from essence. Tools - peace in being, structure within the structureless, "the ability to work from a deeper level of being (off by heart / from essence)".

* Creative visualisation - slow yourself down holding focus on the essence of that which it is you so desire, now bring forth lightly and positively into the now.

* Constructively review.

* Coming from & off essence "is the greatest focal tool (lateral beingness)". Spirit soul allignment.

* Inner child "What advice would the younger you, give you now?".

* Inner adult "What advice would the older, wiser you give you now".

* Enhance lateral beingness. Try not, pushing hinders, but keep focus on, and let it come forth.

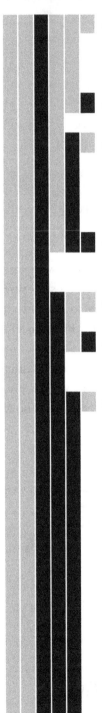

* Untying the knots of the past, as one does so, things take on a more linear nature, as things become linear, a stronger pure-driveness will come to the forefront.

* Transmuting wisdom from knowledge & knowhow.

* Have wisdom but learn to wear it well, as one doesn't need to to pull out wisdom to show one has it and in many cases it may prove to be more useful not to show it.

* The past and present; the building block for the future.

* Light, Free & Easy.

* To be of the fullest, most omnipotent nature possible, "omnipotentiality".

* To have things come from essence is the greatest of constructs; now how does one achieve such?. Sometimes it's not a matter of going forwards, it's a matter of letting go of what is holding you back. Do away with old bad habits of the mass taught collective; rehashing and co-relation may be good tools but there are better ways and greater tools that you know from your spirit sourced individuality- be aware that many visualisations and tools from built up conditioning from others, and collected learning may lay the seeds of the old world rather than a positively alligned healthier spacing and beingness. There is a much greater way if you wish to forge a new path and have the doors open; An essence memory is called for, the doors open, then one becomes consciously aware of some of the subtle more omnipotent natures of the universe. This is

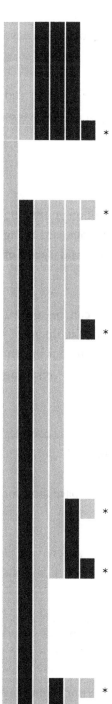

a great process to actuate, the seeds and sands of time will aid and in due course the rewards will be received. Most people have this ability it just requires nurturing and a conscious application of effort.

* It will come into being to be recollected if it's meant to; the more one funds this way of being the easier and lighter it is.

* Learn to free one's memory. Holding on to memory is a good way of losing your greater spirit honed focal stagnation, and tripping over ones thought process, get creative & reapplicate to your own full journey. Sit within the fluctuances and stay light.

* Move away from ie – don't forget, to – I can't remember, to - I do not recall to – always remember, as it helps and creates a slow movement towards better memory (Better Memory Skills). Come up with your own version. Keep life new, fresh and inspired, as the past has brought you to where you are now. Positively & creatively reapply yourself. Relax ~ keep your energy flowing purely and lightly.

* What is the probability of being here NOW?. You are where you are meant to be.

* Change from moment to moment, instant to instant. Stay focally clear & light, as this will enaid full-mind, and forge you on track again with your own individualistic dream of what you have envisaged for yourself.

* Stay positive, clear and clear driven, live life within certifiable faith, and know that truth and purity is

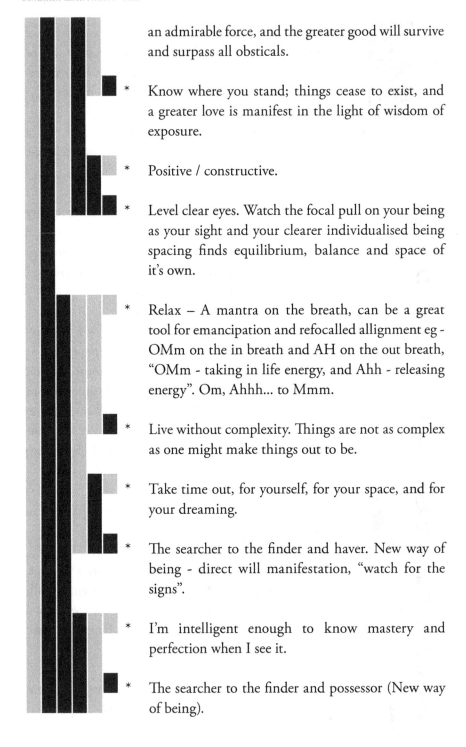

an admirable force, and the greater good will survive and surpass all obsticals.

* Know where you stand; things cease to exist, and a greater love is manifest in the light of wisdom of exposure.

* Positive / constructive.

* Level clear eyes. Watch the focal pull on your being as your sight and your clearer individualised being spacing finds equilibrium, balance and space of it's own.

* Relax – A mantra on the breath, can be a great tool for emancipation and refocalled allignment eg - OMm on the in breath and AH on the out breath, "OMm - taking in life energy, and Ahh - releasing energy". Om, Ahhh... to Mmm.

* Live without complexity. Things are not as complex as one might make things out to be.

* Take time out, for yourself, for your space, and for your dreaming.

* The searcher to the finder and haver. New way of being - direct will manifestation, "watch for the signs".

* I'm intelligent enough to know mastery and perfection when I see it.

* The searcher to the finder and possessor (New way of being).

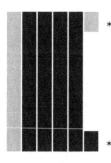

* A better way to remember and bring forth into the now is from an essence of full spirit self. Channel and be a conduit of total recall, while being based in the process of allowing this way of being to manifest and gain strength.

* A healthy application of effort is all that is required; the process will be endured for you if you get out of your own way and do what you can, the universe will go about helping you, as much as you go about helping yourself; stay positive, and nurture being within the greater good.

COLLABORATING

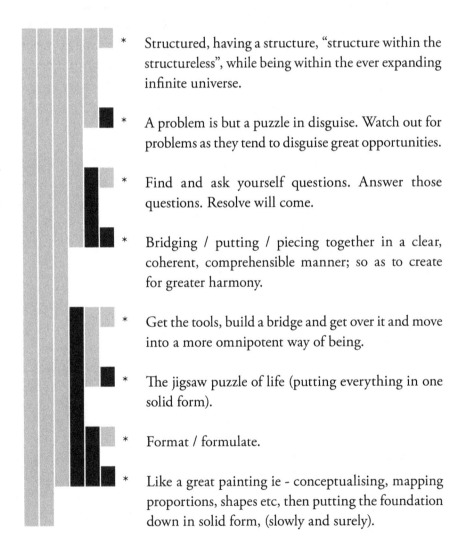

* Structured, having a structure, "structure within the structureless", while being within the ever expanding infinite universe.

* A problem is but a puzzle in disguise. Watch out for problems as they tend to disguise great opportunities.

* Find and ask yourself questions. Answer those questions. Resolve will come.

* Bridging / putting / piecing together in a clear, coherent, comprehensible manner; so as to create for greater harmony.

* Get the tools, build a bridge and get over it and move into a more omnipotent way of being.

* The jigsaw puzzle of life (putting everything in one solid form).

* Format / formulate.

* Like a great painting ie - conceptualising, mapping proportions, shapes etc, then putting the foundation down in solid form, (slowly and surely).

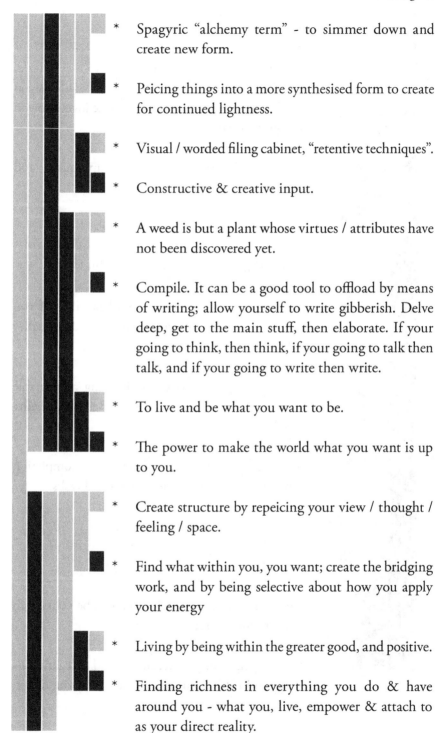

* Spagyric "alchemy term" - to simmer down and create new form.

* Peicing things into a more synthesised form to create for continued lightness.

* Visual / worded filing cabinet, "retentive techniques".

* Constructive & creative input.

* A weed is but a plant whose virtues / attributes have not been discovered yet.

* Compile. It can be a good tool to offload by means of writing; allow yourself to write gibberish. Delve deep, get to the main stuff, then elaborate. If your going to think, then think, if your going to talk then talk, and if your going to write then write.

* To live and be what you want to be.

* The power to make the world what you want is up to you.

* Create structure by repeicing your view / thought / feeling / space.

* Find what within you, you want; create the bridging work, and by being selective about how you apply your energy

* Living by being within the greater good, and positive.

* Finding richness in everything you do & have around you - what you, live, empower & attach to as your direct reality.

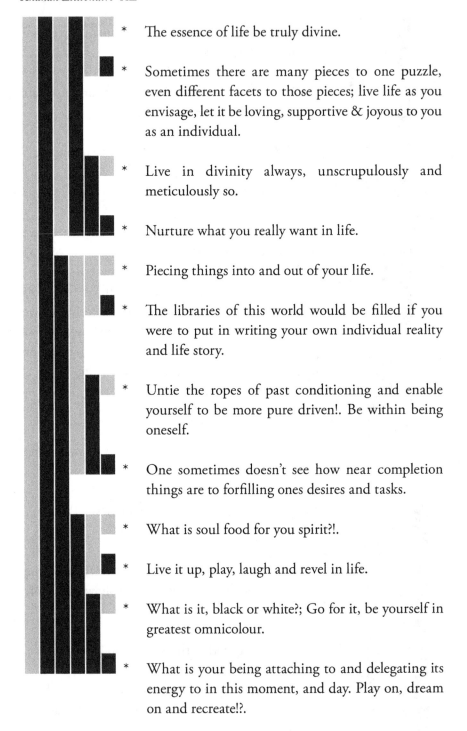

* The essence of life be truly divine.

* Sometimes there are many pieces to one puzzle, even different facets to those pieces; live life as you envisage, let it be loving, supportive & joyous to you as an individual.

* Live in divinity always, unscrupulously and meticulously so.

* Nurture what you really want in life.

* Piecing things into and out of your life.

* The libraries of this world would be filled if you were to put in writing your own individual reality and life story.

* Untie the ropes of past conditioning and enable yourself to be more pure driven!. Be within being oneself.

* One sometimes doesn't see how near completion things are to forfilling ones desires and tasks.

* What is soul food for you spirit?!.

* Live it up, play, laugh and revel in life.

* What is it, black or white?; Go for it, be yourself in greatest omnicolour.

* What is your being attaching to and delegating its energy to in this moment, and day. Play on, dream on and recreate!?.

STRUCTURE
(Foundationary tools)

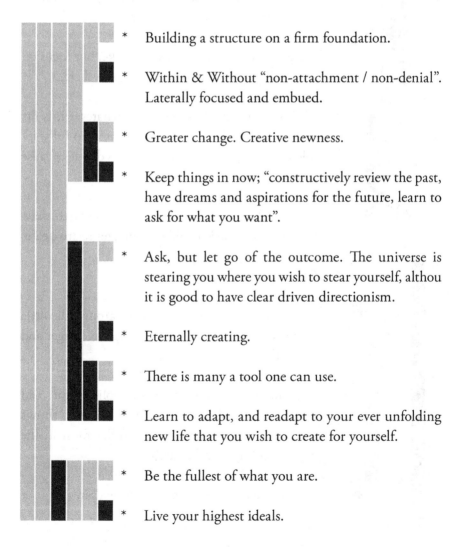

* Building a structure on a firm foundation.

* Within & Without "non-attachment / non-denial". Laterally focused and embued.

* Greater change. Creative newness.

* Keep things in now; "constructively review the past, have dreams and aspirations for the future, learn to ask for what you want".

* Ask, but let go of the outcome. The universe is stearing you where you wish to stear yourself, althou it is good to have clear driven directionism.

* Eternally creating.

* There is many a tool one can use.

* Learn to adapt, and readapt to your ever unfolding new life that you wish to create for yourself.

* Be the fullest of what you are.

* Live your highest ideals.

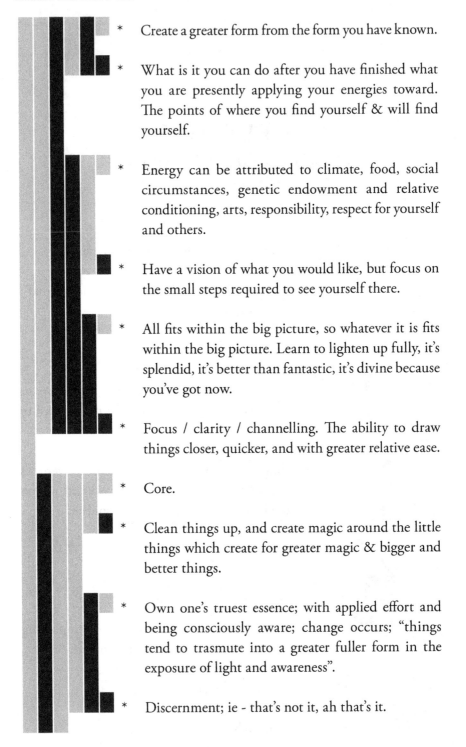

* Create a greater form from the form you have known.

* What is it you can do after you have finished what you are presently applying your energies toward. The points of where you find yourself & will find yourself.

* Energy can be attributed to climate, food, social circumstances, genetic endowment and relative conditioning, arts, responsibility, respect for yourself and others.

* Have a vision of what you would like, but focus on the small steps required to see yourself there.

* All fits within the big picture, so whatever it is fits within the big picture. Learn to lighten up fully, it's splendid, it's better than fantastic, it's divine because you've got now.

* Focus / clarity / channelling. The ability to draw things closer, quicker, and with greater relative ease.

* Core.

* Clean things up, and create magic around the little things which create for greater magic & bigger and better things.

* Own one's truest essence; with applied effort and being consciously aware; change occurs; "things tend to trasmute into a greater fuller form in the exposure of light and awareness".

* Discernment; ie - that's not it, ah that's it.

* Attach to that which fits and leave the rest.

* Yes, it's good to acknowledge, but move on.

* Be it one scrunchy or a million scrunchies, if one doesn't need a scrunchy one doesn't need a scrunchy.

* Crawling along a tunnel; one never loses ground one only ever gains, move and gain greater ground when you can, then relax, and enjoy if you decide to sit in one spot; and if there is a block in one's path, imagine yourself fluid and pass through it.

* Get into sync and harmony now.

* From shades of grey to black and white, it soon turns to colour, and even omnicolour if one looks closely. Create for greater clarity.

* Talk, write, journalise, dictaphone; move away from internalization as this creates for congestion. (move away from analysis paralysis).

* Foundationary work, from the structure of a good home, life & marine green eco friendly planet & living.

* Question & Answer.

* Coming from / at / going to.

* Work is applied effort, "an action program".

* Learn to ask for what you want, and make the footwork towards having that which you desire.

STRUCTURING (Piecing healthy constructs into one's life)

* Within a trip there isn't a trip "one always has one's individualised spirit self". Incorporate one's main fluctuances and trips so as to reharmonise disonant vibrancy patterns; ie - one will then be coming from a more omnipotent spirit soul alligned self, one can flow with the patterning of built up conditioning.

* Put things down before they become heavy and it takes of your energy. A journey may be easier accomplished if one stops for a rest on the way, or steers one's energy elsewhere to reapply energy when it is there. Chipping away, "obstacles will inevitably be removed".

* There is much to be had in where you've come from, where your are at, and where your are heading. Beginning / middle / successful completion "synthesised unified tempest point and being in the deliverance of the full reception".

* Reveal / Re-vealing. Go with the flow, one learns how to steer oneself.

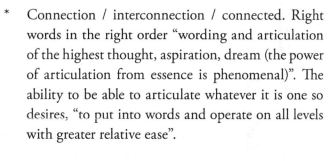

* Connection / interconnection / connected. Right words in the right order "wording and articulation of the highest thought, aspiration, dream (the power of articulation from essence is phenomenal)". The ability to be able to articulate whatever it is one so desires, "to put into words and operate on all levels with greater relative ease".

* Construct and build anew, from the older limited parts of self, create anew, the reward is in itself for yourself. Conceive / perceive / believe / recieve.

* Act as if...eg - it aids in the embrace of where one would like to see oneself. Living life fully unfettered, unrestricted (taking the full you with you).

* Bridging work, "getting rid and moving away from old ways of being that are no longer needed or are outmoded". Ascend, erase, & replace, "walk the solution". New fresh and inspirational, find new wording to express yourself.

* Whatever one can envisage (dream up) is but a peg holding the boat to the endless sea. It all fits within the big picture, it helps one to let go and feed into the bounty of what the universe has to offer, (stepping out of the way as the universe wishes to see you where you wish to see yourself). Immaculate concepts; Infinite and divine scenarios. One can be making up the dream as one goes along. Envisioning the dream; to living the most amazing of any preconceived dream.

* An infusion of elements in fluctuance, flowing peacefully and serenely. Learn to move and sing with the swing & music of life. If things don't fit it may

be best left for a different time in a different space, or maybe not to attach or take it out all together. Intunement / resonance.

* Maybe not knowing what one wants, but knowing what one doesn't want, which clears away the debris, as this may create for room for something new / else to come into the spaces that get created. Addressing & shining light on that which, as in achnologing such will create more room in one's life for the greater more life giving energies to come into your life. What one no longer requires, does not need or fit in your life.

* Yum I want it all to fall in my lap!. I started to make my way up the ally to heaven on earth, that ally soon opened up into a boulevard, other boulevards I may have once envisaged closed off to be a non-existent ally.

* Interrelation, ie - the correlation of relationships, "bridge and create flowing resonance for smoother running". Look in the room uncovering that which may be hidden or laying dormant eg - take the door off, use a candle, the sun, or shine a non-pollutive / renewable1000 watt halogen lamp "Non Pollutive / Renewable / New Free Energy Sources" in there "things will die a natural death through the process creating harmony". The only way to get rid of the old world / outmoded is to yield to it, an assertive self appraisal while validating and having great respect for self, and the better advocating that, that is to come.

* Give to someone of the true love through being true. Repent the fault not the actor of it "call for

46

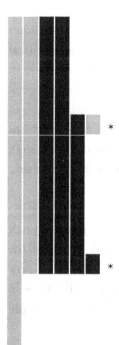

the demanifestation of the fault within one's universe (one may see results happening quickly)". Composting the old, seeing and living the new / good.

* It may be a case of debinding the knot before moving forward. It may be that one has been thrown a rope as one may be in a metaphorical hole, one may be required to pull oneself out, (The universe will help and accommodate those that help and accommodate & empower the solution work for oneself).

* Do not buy what you want but what you need; What one doesn't need is dear at whatever the cost may be, eg - collecting nuts and bolts may create for a situation in which it empowers a purpose for its use (helps clear the way for creating unwanted situations in ones life).

* The short cut may mean one may be required to start from the beginning, "have faith you are where you are meant to be, it's all mighty fine!".

* Ring out the old, ring in the new, ring out the false, ring in the true.

* A journey of a thousand miles begins with one step "once one embarks, a bus, plane or intergalactic spaceshuttler may come and make the trip short". Tools are and can be very enaiding to your journey, but the need for outgrowing ones tools and embracing the newer is insurmountable, ask yourself what is the new, fresh more life giving ground in which to be journeyed within by yourself.

* It may start as addition and subtraction, one soon learns how to multiply and divide etc (A mathematical way of looking at that which fits and aids one in steering ones reality). Head to the heart and back again "Tis a tool to work out what fits", one will then come from a more pure driven & omnipotent way of being. The tools and answers come through such a process. To give time to something may save you a lot more time.

* Live life uninhibitedly full and free "know thy self imposed limitations". Beyond "look at where the map of life has brought you to this point in now land, now would you like to stear yourself and be in the present so as to empower that which you would like in your life.

* Rounding up of concepts etc "bring thing's back to a simplified holistic form / base". From... To... - lower / higher, closed / open, inner / outer. The all encompassing ie - some people have the light on in their house but nothing in it, some have everything in the house but the light off, others have the light on in the house and everything in it (one can have a reality of ones deepest desire inwardly and outwardly)".

* Focal strengths, focus, focusing. Discern greater awareness around the reflective self, nurture the new ground, "knowing where one stands in things, walk and empower the new ground". One never destroys, one only creates (even when one is creating the emancipation and de-manifestation of the old & outmoded). The art of objectification.

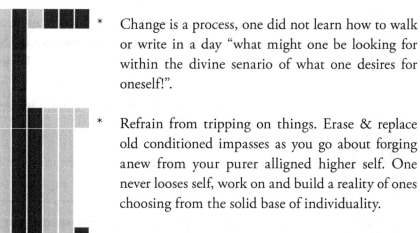

* Change is a process, one did not learn how to walk or write in a day "what might one be looking for within the divine senario of what one desires for oneself!".

* Refrain from tripping on things. Erase & replace old conditioned impasses as you go about forging anew from your purer alligned higher self. One never looses self, work on and build a reality of ones choosing from the solid base of individuality.

* To have resentment or projection on another, is like creating one's own self inflicted baggage. One can set up an auric field "a field of protection" this can be done by visualisation techniques or mantra(s); eg - when moving away from people in a physical sense, pull your energy back to you, raise your hand throwing your energy up and above you (if it's not the place to do it, visualise it), cleanse and lighten your energy, throw away any residual baggage that may not be of benefit to you.

* It can be beneficial to have maps or a base to work from, although creating the map and walking the map may be different.

* Imploring / deliberating "create an opening or room for a change".

* You may need someone or something to rely on. The one thing no one can ever take from you is self. Spirit manifests in all the forms of being; find richness, enjoy all, create and see support in the world around you through having validation of self.

* Resolve your reservations, reservation can impede one's way. Address the small holding factors & enable yourself to get at the main obstacle". Focus on, and invite in the allotment of what you desire in your life inwardly and outwardly. See and find the deliverance of which manifesting.

* Choosing – One may have the choice to go this way or that within each day, both bring different possibilities. One has the choice in every moment, some choices bring far greater rewards than others.

* Being an individual leaf on the same tree of life "embracing one's individuality and the oneness of everything, one always has the individuality of self".

META / NEIVO
(Loving kindness)

* Neivo – The encapsulation / solution of non-violence and the pre-disposed pollar opposite, but in the greater resolve mechanism of only working into the solution, embracing the dualistic while only adhering to the new paradigm from the middle to the greater ground of synergistic life-giving forces.

* To know where one is and where the greater, and more life giving, of things find place within you.

* <u>F</u>ace <u>E</u>verything <u>A</u>nd <u>R</u>ecover / <u>F</u>alse <u>E</u>xistence <u>A</u>ppearing <u>R</u>eal.

* Wizardry / the intermarital arts / adrenaline and ones energy in relation to it. Where does one presently find ones form within such a construct?. Does one wish change or want to change, as in empowering opposition or feeding into dualism one creates such, walk tall, fresh, new and strong. Love, light, truth and purity.

* Tread the new ground and the actuation of a new belief system, your life has brought you to this point now. The willingness to walk anew. The seed of faith that one is eternally looked after.

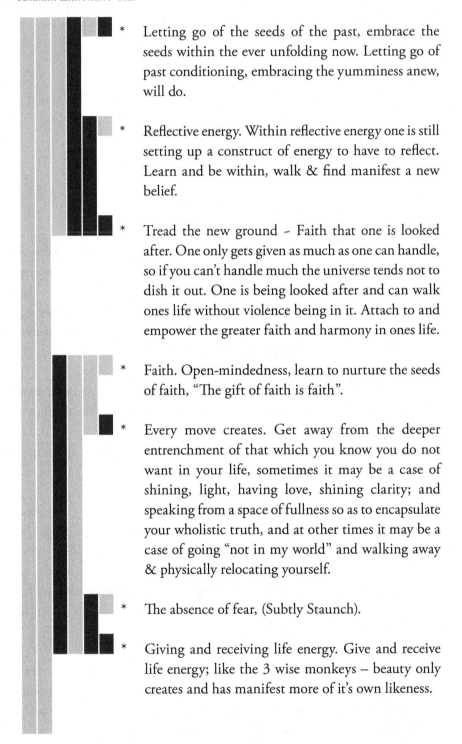

* Letting go of the seeds of the past, embrace the seeds within the ever unfolding now. Letting go of past conditioning, embracing the yumminess anew, will do.

* Reflective energy. Within reflective energy one is still setting up a construct of energy to have to reflect. Learn and be within, walk & find manifest a new belief.

* Tread the new ground ~ Faith that one is looked after. One only gets given as much as one can handle, so if you can't handle much the universe tends not to dish it out. One is being looked after and can walk ones life without violence being in it. Attach to and empower the greater faith and harmony in ones life.

* Faith. Open-mindedness, learn to nurture the seeds of faith, "The gift of faith is faith".

* Every move creates. Get away from the deeper entrenchment of that which you know you do not want in your life, sometimes it may be a case of shining, light, having love, shining clarity; and speaking from a space of fullness so as to encapsulate your wholistic truth, and at other times it may be a case of going "not in my world" and walking away & physically relocating yourself.

* The absence of fear, (Subtly Staunch).

* Giving and receiving life energy. Give and receive life energy; like the 3 wise monkeys – beauty only creates and has manifest more of it's own likeness.

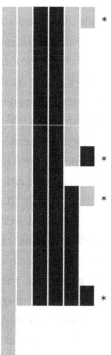

* One doesn't need to carry unnecessary baggage, throw the energy off, ground yourself and bring your energy back up. As one lets unwanted influences in, one may project less than constructively onto oneself, others & / or the world around you; Pull yourself up and activate the solution.

* Abundantly giving greater life energy.

* Move into - unridgid, unprojected, dynamically flowing, life energy. Resolve by being in the solution and grow. Forge the creative, fertile, life giving energy in your life and in the lives of those around you.

* Love and give what you can. Respect - how would you like to be treated?. Do onto others as you would that they should onto you, thinking of the other person as yourself, and tis also a better space to be coming from within respecting an others centred space". Be respectful love & give what you can where its not taking from yourself or that of another.

* How would you like the world around you to be "A wall in one person's path is but a stepping stone on another's path".

* Be clear, vigilant and diligent. Healing and clearing as you go.

* A rung in a ladder is only to be rested upon aiding one to get somewhat higher. Each step generates momentum.

* To do what it takes. We live in a world where collectively and as while being within individuality we can heal, educate, reforest, fix in a very positive

way this world before us (Earth). Tis also good to respect the vestiges of the individual dreamtimes, no matter what the justification and rationalization are as the freedommakers go about de-slaving those kept and held by the old world and spaces. The free new world and inhabitants, some things in this society have been detracting from the greater health and life energy for to long, which has been denying and inhibiting our greater god given pre-birth rite. We individually are entitled to work through the dynamic play of the universal winds and full god creator self to conduct the dream world, one of billion year old synergistic inherent fullness, this is non infringing as there is a big process to the conduction of such. It may be as near as turning around the side of a molecule of an atom to find you are in the dream world beyond belief. :-) Tweet, tweet, - for the little birdies and rainforrest I said personally I'd do that which i can and help save, protect & re-grow.

* Own ones truest essence nature, things will naturally flow as water tends to find its level.

* Meta – peaceful resistance / love flow of goodness, passivity, peace, love within communication "voice box and other", greater understanding, and communion with the greater nature & synergies of is'ness creating and empowering that which you do.

* Live your knowing, forge anew – you don't know it all and some things may take a long time to master.

* Do and be what you want to be to the fullest, as long as it's giving of the love and life energy, & coming from a space of pure motive.

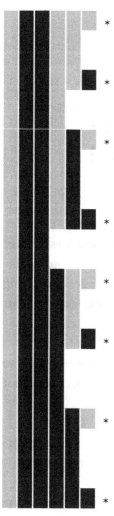

* Own your fullest self, past life ascension, and future life manifesting; the tools will come to you. ☺

* Phew, for a moment in a space of linear time I was starting to...... H'Ra - where am I now?.

* Not much to go now. You have, and the world has come along way, "Individually, in part and healthily". Go the dreamtimes, especially fairy world!.

* So where to from here, should I ...., or should I ....? Hmmm, H'yommm, H'yummmideeeeeeee...

* Temperance - even tempered inner sanctity of spirit soul alligned full self.

* What is your highest ideal?, Live it, walk free dear child of the universe and embrace what it is you want.

* Emancipate the old, embrace the new, baby steps and giant leaps - get those creative, fertile, rich life giving juices flowing.

* Clarity, resolve, lightness, enrapturement and oneness.

PULLING ONESELF UP
(Living in the solution)

* Two men look out to the same view, one sees garbage the other sees stars. The power to transmute objects of design through the force of greater life giving energy. Create your own picture and view of what your own individualised life is.

* That's not it... "know thy self"; One needs tools to build a bridge, you already have the tools so why not build a bridge.

* I am all I perceive "one finger out three back". Conceive and perceive change to receive change.

* To ask and let go of the outcome, the universe essentially wants that which one desires for oneself. Remaining open to change and new possibilities.

* Beauty only attracts and has manifest more of its own likeness.

* Get with the solution. A problem is but a puzzle in disguise. Watch out for big problems as they tend to hide many a great opportunity.

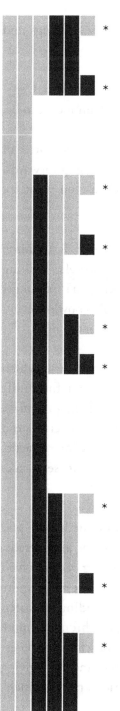

* Work on that which holds you back or limits you. A stitch in time saves nine (Freeing oneself up)".

* Change is a process and generally not an event, one didn't learn to walk or write straight away it took time, willingness and applied effort. Move on, grow, forge & be anew.

* Nurture oneself. Bubba steps, and giants leaps. Keep on keeping on. Bounce Back.

* Live in the now. Keep things in now as there is much to be found in the now "the eternal now of being (Joie de vivre)".

* Clear one's mind.

* Whatever it is, it all fits, and is in flow and harmony!. Work on disonant energy patterns that may be limiting one, it gives room for the door to open for either - something to be set free as it no longer has place in ones life, or for something to come through that awareness into ones life.

* Reveal "ask and one will receive". Bring things back to a simplified form, everything's going to be all scrumdiddlyumshcio.

* Self esteem "love oneself". Have a strong self validation.

* Baby steps or a giant's leap "a wall in one persons path is but a stepping stone on another's path". Open up, give and be love, shake free. Remember to give thanks and acknowledge the universe for

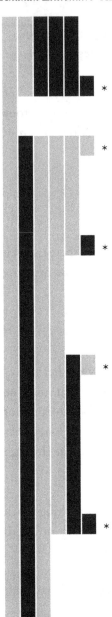

the smallest to the greatest of life's offerings and continued bestowments.

* Things are going as they should. Back to basics, eg – the breath. Faith that I am where I am meant to be.

* More will be revealed. Sometimes it's a matter of letting something go. Rather than going forwards, create openings for the sort of life you want for yourself.

* Move / get away from the deeper ingraining; eg - words, ideology, outmoded beliefs, limiting constructs of self and ways of being that no longer serves one as your higher self. Acknowledge but move on, & empower the solution in the now.

* Getting away from... Ascending that which causes dis-ease, or does not fit as your future life (non -empowerment through attachment or denial), have a healthy focus. Steering oneself in better stead in the future "grab the throttle of the intergalactic, multidymentionional spacesurfing of self, take control".

* <u>HOW</u> - <u>H</u>onesty, <u>O</u>pen-mindedness and <u>W</u>illingness. A lie is but the truth in masquerade, it is just a greater synergistic working of that which is, showing a convergence of forces that may require greater compassion and understanding. Greater, purer alignments of one's energies through a more wholesome truth. Be in greater conscious awareness of that which is in play, and generate more life-giving nectars of yumminess like peace and happiness. Know yourself.

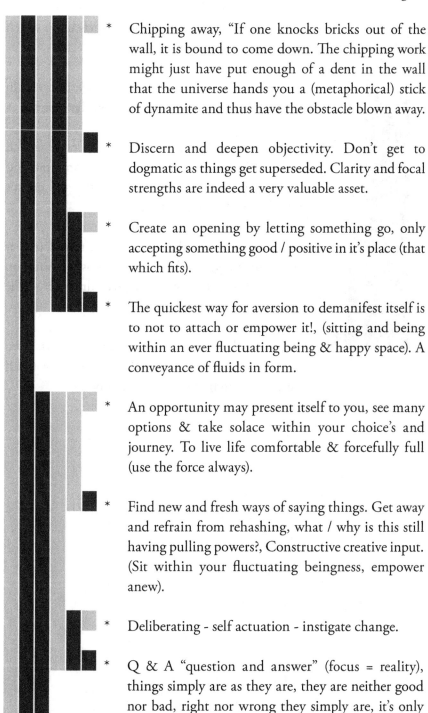

* Chipping away, "If one knocks bricks out of the wall, it is bound to come down. The chipping work might just have put enough of a dent in the wall that the universe hands you a (metaphorical) stick of dynamite and thus have the obstacle blown away.

* Discern and deepen objectivity. Don't get to dogmatic as things get superseded. Clarity and focal strengths are indeed a very valuable asset.

* Create an opening by letting something go, only accepting something good / positive in it's place (that which fits).

* The quickest way for aversion to demanifest itself is to not to attach or empower it!, (sitting and being within an ever fluctuating being & happy space). A conveyance of fluids in form.

* An opportunity may present itself to you, see many options & take solace within your choice's and journey. To live life comfortable & forcefully full (use the force always).

* Find new and fresh ways of saying things. Get away and refrain from rehashing, what / why is this still having pulling powers?, Constructive creative input. (Sit within your fluctuating beingness, empower anew).

* Deliberating - self actuation - instigate change.

* Q & A "question and answer" (focus = reality), things simply are as they are, they are neither good nor bad, right nor wrong they simply are, it's only ones attachment around these things that gives it

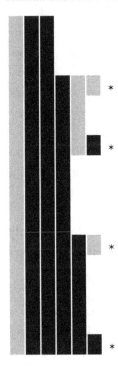

place or credence. They are but models upon which one can remould oneself on.

* Where might one like to see oneself, getting within the solution rather than dwelling on the past.

* Having no closed doors "being open, true and full within being, one then becomes omnipresent, omnipotent and opens the door to the god creator within". Blossoming respect.

* Foundation work - build on solid ground (rather than quicksand and lose it all), choose to build on granite with 1 km titanium poles driven into the ground.

* Pull yourself out of present holes, the rope has been thrown to you, your requirement is to pull yourself out; "It has to be a self actuated process".

HARMONY / HAPPINESS

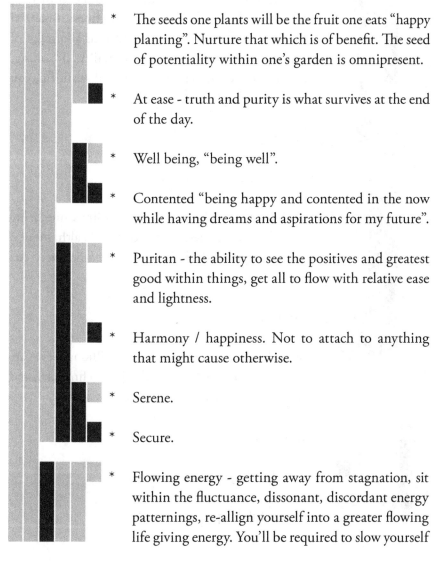

* The seeds one plants will be the fruit one eats "happy planting". Nurture that which is of benefit. The seed of potentiality within one's garden is omnipresent.

* At ease - truth and purity is what survives at the end of the day.

* Well being, "being well".

* Contented "being happy and contented in the now while having dreams and aspirations for my future".

* Puritan - the ability to see the positives and greatest good within things, get all to flow with relative ease and lightness.

* Harmony / happiness. Not to attach to anything that might cause otherwise.

* Serene.

* Secure.

* Flowing energy - getting away from stagnation, sit within the fluctuance, dissonant, discordant energy patternings, re-allign yourself into a greater flowing life giving energy. You'll be required to slow yourself

61

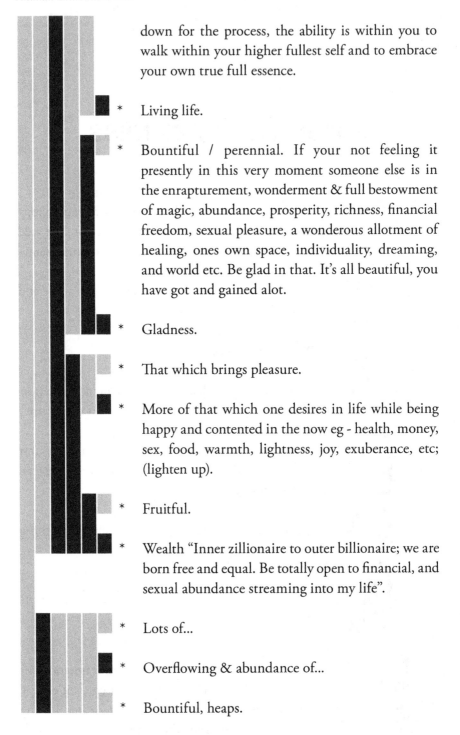

down for the process, the ability is within you to walk within your higher fullest self and to embrace your own true full essence.

* Living life.

* Bountiful / perennial. If your not feeling it presently in this very moment someone else is in the enrapturement, wonderment & full bestowment of magic, abundance, prosperity, richness, financial freedom, sexual pleasure, a wonderous allotment of healing, ones own space, individuality, dreaming, and world etc. Be glad in that. It's all beautiful, you have got and gained alot.

* Gladness.

* That which brings pleasure.

* More of that which one desires in life while being happy and contented in the now eg - health, money, sex, food, warmth, lightness, joy, exuberance, etc; (lighten up).

* Fruitful.

* Wealth "Inner zillionaire to outer billionaire; we are born free and equal. Be totally open to financial, and sexual abundance streaming into my life".

* Lots of...

* Overflowing & abundance of...

* Bountiful, heaps.

* More than enough.

* A harvest of love, understanding, provodential bestowment of yummy energy, coming into ones life freely and easily.

* Very beautiful / Appealing.

* Warm fuzzies.

* Abundance.

* Copious.

* Oodles.

* Fulfilled / Full.

* Satisfied.

* Heaven on earth "as above so below, what would you like to see manifest before you?".

* Universally universal "from the smallest flower to the tallest tree", bring all into greater clarity; Starts from self then ripple it outwards. From the inside out, to the outside in.

* Ecstatically oozing life giving energies?!.

* Divinely divine, just walking the walk, purity of my bestowments, love to you all XO Az.

PEACE

* Doors are opening and obstacles are being swept aside.

* Free, light and at ease.

* The shells of the past hold the seeds of now.

* Change ones approach to constructively reviewing the past and the now one currently finds oneself in. Let the outlook of the future to be positive. Enjoy the full embodiment of the greater more life giving life.

* Bring things back to a simplified form.

* Peace - essential essence state of being, if it isn't there simplify, eg - living the eternal now of being as best one can etc.

* At-ease-ment.

* Freedom.

* Having a being of contentment on all levels, "mind, body, soul, spirit".

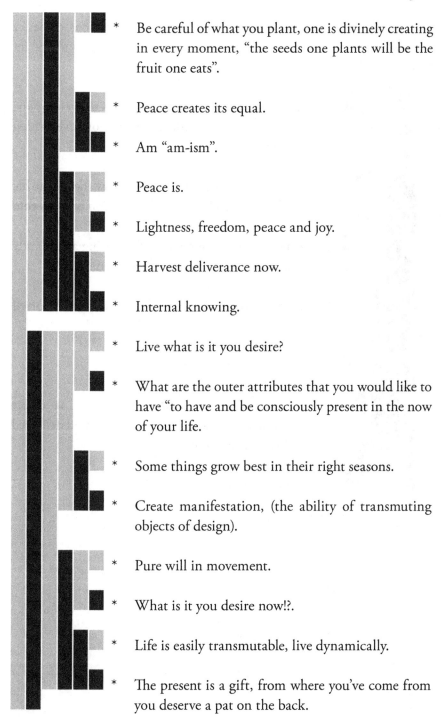

* Be careful of what you plant, one is divinely creating in every moment, "the seeds one plants will be the fruit one eats".

* Peace creates its equal.

* Am "am-ism".

* Peace is.

* Lightness, freedom, peace and joy.

* Harvest deliverance now.

* Internal knowing.

* Live what is it you desire?

* What are the outer attributes that you would like to have "to have and be consciously present in the now of your life.

* Some things grow best in their right seasons.

* Create manifestation, (the ability of transmuting objects of design).

* Pure will in movement.

* What is it you desire now!?.

* Life is easily transmutable, live dynamically.

* The present is a gift, from where you've come from you deserve a pat on the back.

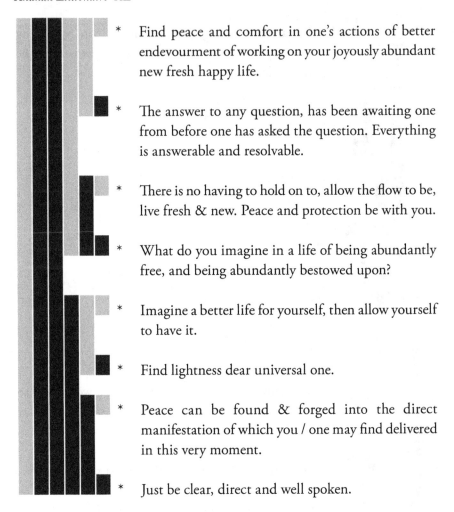

* Find peace and comfort in one's actions of better endevourment of working on your joyously abundant new fresh happy life.

* The answer to any question, has been awaiting one from before one has asked the question. Everything is answerable and resolvable.

* There is no having to hold on to, allow the flow to be, live fresh & new. Peace and protection be with you.

* What do you imagine in a life of being abundantly free, and being abundantly bestowed upon?

* Imagine a better life for yourself, then allow yourself to have it.

* Find lightness dear universal one.

* Peace can be found & forged into the direct manifestation of which you / one may find delivered in this very moment.

* Just be clear, direct and well spoken.

POSITIVE / CONSTRUCTIVE

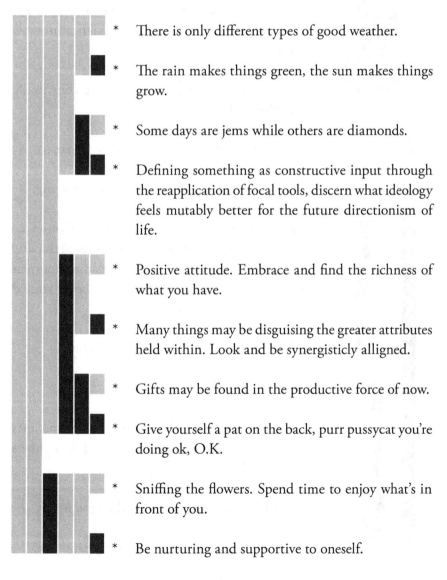

* There is only different types of good weather.

* The rain makes things green, the sun makes things grow.

* Some days are jems while others are diamonds.

* Defining something as constructive input through the reapplication of focal tools, discern what ideology feels mutably better for the future directionism of life.

* Positive attitude. Embrace and find the richness of what you have.

* Many things may be disguising the greater attributes held within. Look and be synergisticly alligned.

* Gifts may be found in the productive force of now.

* Give yourself a pat on the back, purr pussycat you're doing ok, O.K.

* Sniffing the flowers. Spend time to enjoy what's in front of you.

* Be nurturing and supportive to oneself.

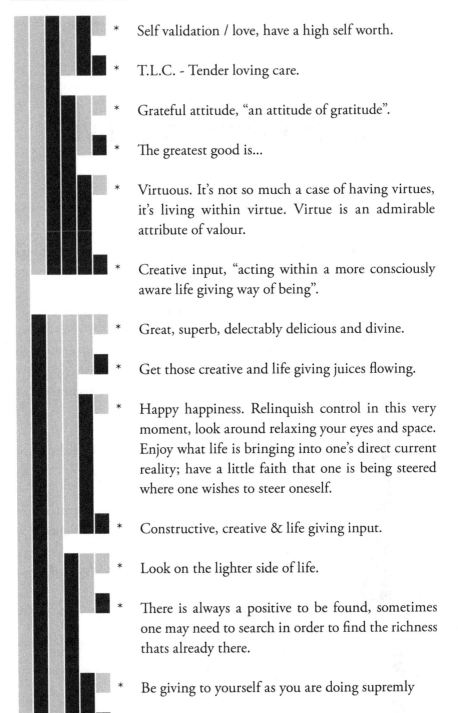

* Self validation / love, have a high self worth.

* T.L.C. - Tender loving care.

* Grateful attitude, "an attitude of gratitude".

* The greatest good is...

* Virtuous. It's not so much a case of having virtues, it's living within virtue. Virtue is an admirable attribute of valour.

* Creative input, "acting within a more consciously aware life giving way of being".

* Great, superb, delectably delicious and divine.

* Get those creative and life giving juices flowing.

* Happy happiness. Relinquish control in this very moment, look around relaxing your eyes and space. Enjoy what life is bringing into one's direct current reality; have a little faith that one is being steered where one wishes to steer oneself.

* Constructive, creative & life giving input.

* Look on the lighter side of life.

* There is always a positive to be found, sometimes one may need to search in order to find the richness thats already there.

* Be giving to yourself as you are doing supremly

* This is not a place as much as it is a perspective.

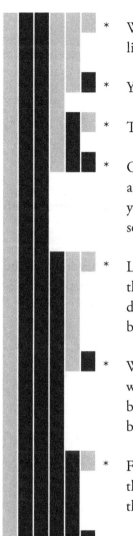

* We can only change our reality, (transforming our lives) in the split second that is our now.

* You can live it and have it as part of your life.

* The simplest way is to be.

* Operate within the mutables. This will empower a richness one may find in deliverance later on, if you were to choose to make a decision to enact the solution.

* Living it, by slowly incorporating and adapting through positive, fresh, re-attachments and healthy discernment. It will aid you in the perpetuation of beneficial outcomes in your life.

* Walk the fresher newer more life-giving ground while keeping a foundation of what has come to be you & your life in the present day / moment before me.

* Flow with oneness, within the polarity of polarising things - attachment can be a holding force keeping things in your life.

* Take time to enjoy the small things in life!.

CLARITY

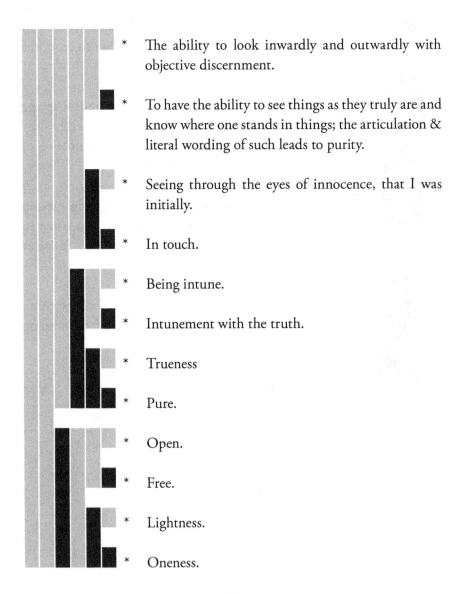

* The ability to look inwardly and outwardly with objective discernment.

* To have the ability to see things as they truly are and know where one stands in things; the articulation & literal wording of such leads to purity.

* Seeing through the eyes of innocence, that I was initially.

* In touch.

* Being intune.

* Intunement with the truth.

* Trueness

* Pure.

* Open.

* Free.

* Lightness.

* Oneness.

* In sync.

* Full vessel.

* High resonance.

* Walking, living and being free.

* Full clarity and your own individualised uncompramised space.

* Walking talking and being freely, telling ones truth & reality as you see it.

* Operate without puppet strings attached around one's hands and feet, mind and space.

* The ability to speak one's truth clearly and concisely telling it as it is.

* Conveyance of your visualisation with another of the dynamic beings of the universe.

* To feel fresh and renewed.

* Move in conscious growth. Become more consciously aware of that which is your current life.

* I thought if only the chance wasn't one in a trillion to the power of infinite billions!. Immeasurable calculations get surpassed and proven to be highly synergistic and greater of the paradym of self. The chance is there living its own existence in form eg - like a parallel world or existence - whether one turns left or right it is there, in form, living it's own

existence unperturbed and free from the constraints of your previously built up conditioning.

* Things become clear when one knows where one is within things.

* Write a pro's and con's list of whatever is of importance to you or is of the greatest influence in your life. Through the process and after the process one will gain clarity. The process helps to put things in perspective & enaids for a clearer allignment of where you emplace your focal powers for future directionism and subtle seed planting of which you will reap the harvest of in time yet had.

* You are where you are ment to be, everything has brought you to this point in now land, creatively cultivate and nurture the spacesurfing of where you would like to be & see as life and your dreaming. See the manifestation of such in this day that is your own individually appointed dream life. Be that, and embrace the omnipotentiality of provodencial bestowments, living true to your higher form and that which it brings.

* Slowly and surely - it's a process not an event, by pointing your feet in the right direction or chipping away you'll be surprised how much time and effort it will save. Your journey will and is being helped out & enaided in many ways!.

* Apply conscious effort now may save you multitudes of extra effort, applied effort love.

* Clarity is simply being more consciously aware, and the ability of how to use & apply greater conscious

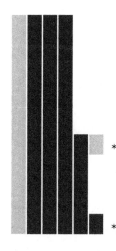

awareness. There is greatness within fullness. Be clear, light and in sync "The peacemaker". Your will can & is determinedfrom moment to greater unfoldment. Create a new paradigm for yourself. Enter and live your dream reality.

* Stick to the up's and that which is positive input in your life, get rid of that which no longer serves your life.

* An essence of articulating ones being, sharpening images.

UNIVERSAL REALITY

* The big picture "energy, people, life, your dreams and fantasies..., are all but a small piece of the forever and possibilities of all that is.

* Synergistically aligned with the greater dream times and worlds within worlds, sometimes one may need to let go of something and see it demanifested, in order to be given passage to another world, "rites of passage".

* The history of conditioned existence is but a map and guide for your future life and living.

* Open the door to anything perceivable is possible. There is my truth, your truth & then there is the truth. Forge & create greater refined alignment, and discard outmoded ways that no longer support. The brave new free world. We forge and get greater knowledge of what that is, as we go along.

* Difficult things take time, impossible things take longer, & can be looked at as being in the world of infinite probabilities.

* Be not interested in the possibilities of defeat, be around supportive people, keep a high light, and life giving energy yourself.

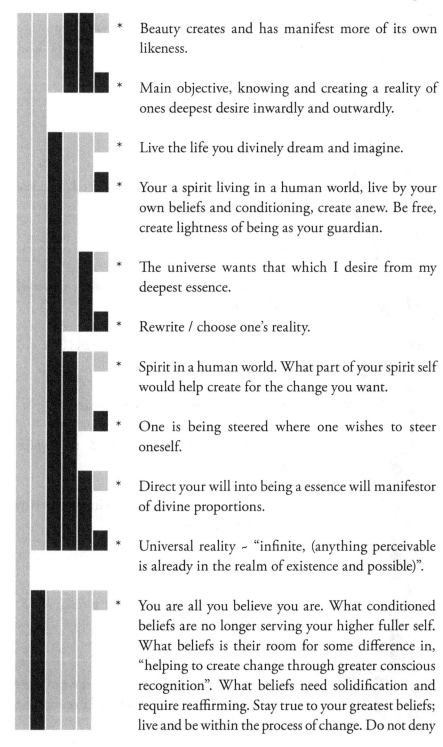

* Beauty creates and has manifest more of its own likeness.

* Main objective, knowing and creating a reality of ones deepest desire inwardly and outwardly.

* Live the life you divinely dream and imagine.

* Your a spirit living in a human world, live by your own beliefs and conditioning, create anew. Be free, create lightness of being as your guardian.

* The universe wants that which I desire from my deepest essence.

* Rewrite / choose one's reality.

* Spirit in a human world. What part of your spirit self would help create for the change you want.

* One is being steered where one wishes to steer oneself.

* Direct your will into being a essence will manifestor of divine proportions.

* Universal reality ~ "infinite, (anything perceivable is already in the realm of existence and possible)".

* You are all you believe you are. What conditioned beliefs are no longer serving your higher fuller self. What beliefs is their room for some difference in, "helping to create change through greater conscious recognition". What beliefs need solidification and require reaffirming. Stay true to your greatest beliefs; live and be within the process of change. Do not deny

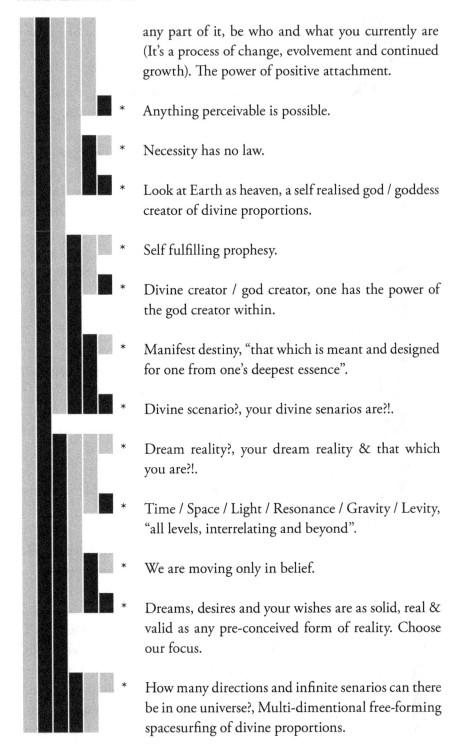

any part of it, be who and what you currently are (It's a process of change, evolvement and continued growth). The power of positive attachment.

* Anything perceivable is possible.

* Necessity has no law.

* Look at Earth as heaven, a self realised god / goddess creator of divine proportions.

* Self fulfilling prophesy.

* Divine creator / god creator, one has the power of the god creator within.

* Manifest destiny, "that which is meant and designed for one from one's deepest essence".

* Divine scenario?, your divine senarios are?!.

* Dream reality?, your dream reality & that which you are?!.

* Time / Space / Light / Resonance / Gravity / Levity, "all levels, interrelating and beyond".

* We are moving only in belief.

* Dreams, desires and your wishes are as solid, real & valid as any pre-conceived form of reality. Choose our focus.

* How many directions and infinite senarios can there be in one universe?, Multi-dimentional free-forming spacesurfing of divine proportions.

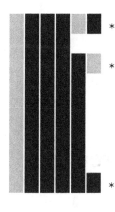

* It's all one.

* There is a wide spectrum of other perceptions that you could have chosen, all of them useful, all and none of them true. There is no paradox & total paradox to everything; beauty within the blossoming nature within the art of things.

* My home is a universe, where the circumference is no-where and the centre is everywhere, and no–time, no–space, and everytime, everyspace. :-)

RELATIVE REALITY
(Conscious building block reality)

* Love, light, purity, harmony, magic, bestowments, provodence...

* Live life fearlessly, unfettered and unrestricted.

* Live the dream life. Build castles in the sky, now go about linking heaven and earth; putting the foundation under your huge plans to give it a strong firmament to rest apon.

* To love fully, glowing energeticly muchly is to be shared & bestowed as within living the great love.

* This above all ~ to thy self be true, steer ones reality using and owning the full spectrum of self. A lie is but the truth in masquerade, or a greater working of that which is, tis favourable to be and surround yourself around that which is more purely alligned to the life you are to have and see manifest perfectly.

* Challenge by looking into one's greatest belief's.

* Looking at life and living as an overflowing bountiful cup of abundance. You are the most beautiful of all the essences. Attach to that which is positive and

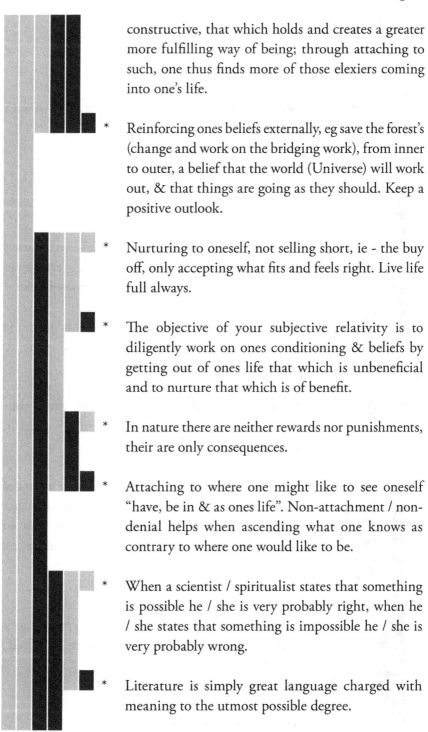

constructive, that which holds and creates a greater more fulfilling way of being; through attaching to such, one thus finds more of those elexiers coming into one's life.

* Reinforcing ones beliefs externally, eg save the forest's (change and work on the bridging work), from inner to outer, a belief that the world (Universe) will work out, & that things are going as they should. Keep a positive outlook.

* Nurturing to oneself, not selling short, ie - the buy off, only accepting what fits and feels right. Live life full always.

* The objective of your subjective relativity is to diligently work on ones conditioning & beliefs by getting out of ones life that which is unbeneficial and to nurture that which is of benefit.

* In nature there are neither rewards nor punishments, their are only consequences.

* Attaching to where one might like to see oneself "have, be in & as ones life". Non-attachment / non-denial helps when ascending what one knows as contrary to where one would like to be.

* When a scientist / spiritualist states that something is possible he / she is very probably right, when he / she states that something is impossible he / she is very probably wrong.

* Literature is simply great language charged with meaning to the utmost possible degree.

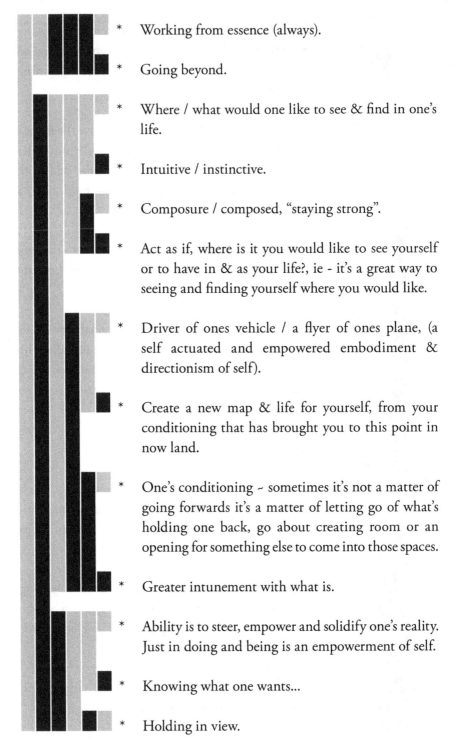

* Working from essence (always).

* Going beyond.

* Where / what would one like to see & find in one's life.

* Intuitive / instinctive.

* Composure / composed, "staying strong".

* Act as if, where is it you would like to see yourself or to have in & as your life?, ie - it's a great way to seeing and finding yourself where you would like.

* Driver of ones vehicle / a flyer of ones plane, (a self actuated and empowered embodiment & directionism of self).

* Create a new map & life for yourself, from your conditioning that has brought you to this point in now land.

* One's conditioning ~ sometimes it's not a matter of going forwards it's a matter of letting go of what's holding one back, go about creating room or an opening for something else to come into those spaces.

* Greater intunement with what is.

* Ability is to steer, empower and solidify one's reality. Just in doing and being is an empowerment of self.

* Knowing what one wants...

* Holding in view.

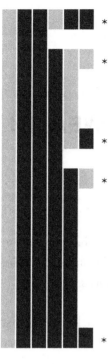

* Nurture the creator within.

* Deepest belief system, "one is ones own deepest belief system, so what are the beliefs you wish to build your life around".

* Every move creates, "creatively visualise".

* To not speak in words is to miss the chance to talk. Better well-intentioned speaking than silence, if you're going to talk, talk; and if you're going to sit in silence sit in silence. It's one of the many blessings; one was given a voice box & a body for a reason how are you going to use it. You wouldn't have preferred to have been born into a reality of silence?!.

* Communication ~ the conveyance and deliverance of thought, vision and subject transference from one to that of another, 'interrelation / one on one / small group / another & others (clear communication with oneself)".

CREATING & CULTIVATING WEALTH

* Increase your energy and output.

* To be very rich you are going to have to accept that you are going to be slightly abnormal. Get committed to yourself and your ideas.

* Be very forceful in buying into richness of that which you wish to create for yourself. Each advance generates momentum.

* It may be less easy to ask for backing and support if you don't support yourself. Have a positive attitude and look at previous successes.

* Hold dear those that are supportive & conducive to your journey & future directionism. You have the divine right to choose with whom you will play and under what circumstances. By eliminating any energy drag the positive good things in your life will manifest faster and easier.

* Power of self grants. If you touch someone does that person make you feel up, positive & happy etc, "what's the first feeling that comes up" now how do you reapply your energies in regards to relationships in your life and what is of importance to get in full power.

* Some people have a lot of built up conditioning that may not be aligned as much as that of those simular to yourself. Some people are more conducive & more wholely alligned to your future journey than others.

* Direct your will into an essence of finely tuned focused intention to help bring about your individualised dreaming. Becoming happily abundant and rich is a moment to moment experience. By my power and the powers that are within this synthesising universe that I am creating the world in which I want as life.

* Use good advice of others you have encountered and will encounter for your future living & life.

* By giving, being loving & nurturing yourself, you are more able to give of your love and learning for another / others.

* <u>WAM</u> - <u>W</u>hat <u>A</u>bout <u>Me</u>. Be nice, fair, and true to your own worth, stating what you would like at the front end. Remember that you are a innocent good and positive child of the universe and all that good stuff.

* Another's success is an affirmation of abundance. To make your plan magic, dynamic, providential and alive touch it daily, this is a form of meditation in which the essence of your being, empowers your plan.

* What gives the eagle its power is its superb sight, not so much its talons, although its talons are a valuable asset for the world in which the eagle lives. A good story needs an end, rather than dribbling off without going anyplace.

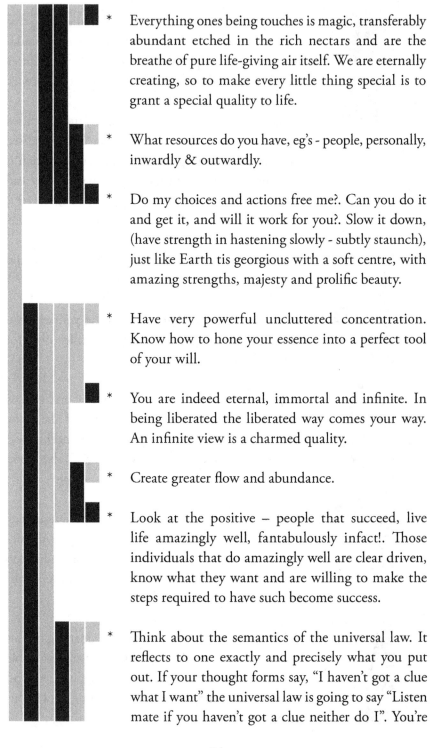

* Everything ones being touches is magic, transferably abundant etched in the rich nectars and are the breathe of pure life-giving air itself. We are eternally creating, so to make every little thing special is to grant a special quality to life.

* What resources do you have, eg's - people, personally, inwardly & outwardly.

* Do my choices and actions free me?. Can you do it and get it, and will it work for you?. Slow it down, (have strength in hastening slowly - subtly staunch), just like Earth tis georgious with a soft centre, with amazing strengths, majesty and prolific beauty.

* Have very powerful uncluttered concentration. Know how to hone your essence into a perfect tool of your will.

* You are indeed eternal, immortal and infinite. In being liberated the liberated way comes your way. An infinite view is a charmed quality.

* Create greater flow and abundance.

* Look at the positive – people that succeed, live life amazingly well, fantabulously infact!. Those individuals that do amazingly well are clear driven, know what they want and are willing to make the steps required to have such become success.

* Think about the semantics of the universal law. It reflects to one exactly and precisely what you put out. If your thought forms say, "I haven't got a clue what I want" the universal law is going to say "Listen mate if you haven't got a clue neither do I". You're

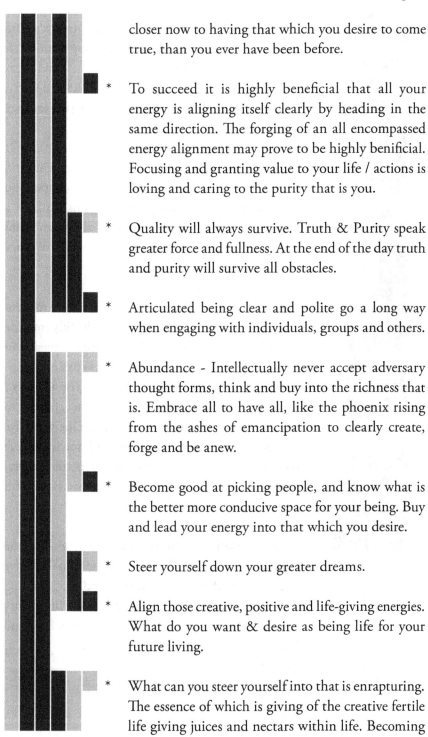

closer now to having that which you desire to come true, than you ever have been before.

* To succeed it is highly beneficial that all your energy is aligning itself clearly by heading in the same direction. The forging of an all encompassed energy alignment may prove to be highly benificial. Focusing and granting value to your life / actions is loving and caring to the purity that is you.

* Quality will always survive. Truth & Purity speak greater force and fullness. At the end of the day truth and purity will survive all obstacles.

* Articulated being clear and polite go a long way when engaging with individuals, groups and others.

* Abundance - Intellectually never accept adversary thought forms, think and buy into the richness that is. Embrace all to have all, like the phoenix rising from the ashes of emancipation to clearly create, forge and be anew.

* Become good at picking people, and know what is the better more conducive space for your being. Buy and lead your energy into that which you desire.

* Steer yourself down your greater dreams.

* Align those creative, positive and life-giving energies. What do you want & desire as being life for your future living.

* What can you steer yourself into that is enrapturing. The essence of which is giving of the creative fertile life giving juices and nectars within life. Becoming

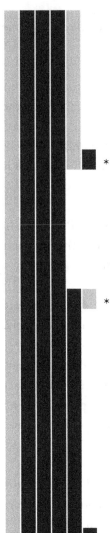

laden with greater artistry is to use the resources and tools one possesses to put one in a strong position (It may mean that you have clarity, awareness and focus that few possess). Virtues, valour, ethics, integrety, respect, valour, etc; go a long way in this journey of life.

* There is no limit to human achievement and endeavour. In committing your plan to paper you solidify it. The written plan functions both as a tool for order and clarity and is an alignment onto your universal go given pre-birth right of your individuality of self.

* The supply is infinite and there will always be more to be received in life if one opens up to it. Buy into the flow of abundance. Breath, live and be lightness. Put yourself in the person you desire, now ask questions or pertinent trigger words, now vessel the answers / solutions. Keep a light flowing resonance, try not to buy into fluctuations or discordance. One will have a greater beingness with the person knowing where thoughts connect to feelings and a better general connection with one's essence beingness. Be careful with who you attach yourself to.

* Pace yourself, be brave and stay within the manifestation of your dream reality. Unusual creative originality within your own in-tuited wisdom. Tap into the parts of the world that create the life energy within, enabling you "that which creates flow and happiness in the process of ones life". Live it, be it, do it. Go for it.

MONEY
(Trade Energy)

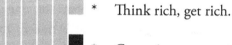

* Think rich, get rich.

* Commit energy to something that you can trade / swap for cash (or vice-versa).

* Money readily flows towards stability, and security.

* Become highly financial, and abundant. Spaces and directionism. Concentrate on the moment, day, month and year. Incorporate a greater amalgimation of financial wealth, tools and the living arts. Forge, live and be financial.

* In committing your plan to paper you make it sacred. The written plan can function as a tool for order, clarity and focal strengths. It is also a prair onto the sanctity of self and enaids creating a clear indication of where you're at, and where your going to. The moves that may best serve and suit you, to find yourself where you want to be.

* I'm committed to safeguarding / protecting and building apon financial wealth, large amounts of money, assets, property, and artistry.

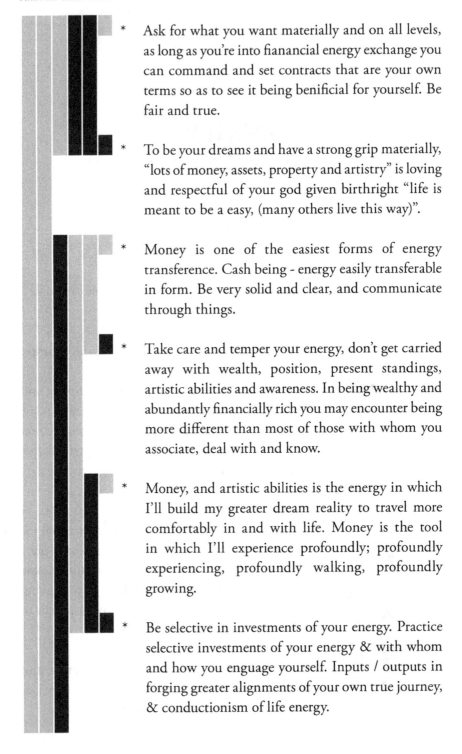

* Ask for what you want materially and on all levels, as long as you're into fianancial energy exchange you can command and set contracts that are your own terms so as to see it being benificial for yourself. Be fair and true.

* To be your dreams and have a strong grip materially, "lots of money, assets, property and artistry" is loving and respectful of your god given birthright "life is meant to be a easy, (many others live this way)".

* Money is one of the easiest forms of energy transference. Cash being - energy easily transferable in form. Be very solid and clear, and communicate through things.

* Take care and temper your energy, don't get carried away with wealth, position, present standings, artistic abilities and awareness. In being wealthy and abundantly fianancially rich you may encounter being more different than most of those with whom you associate, deal with and know.

* Money, and artistic abilities is the energy in which I'll build my greater dream reality to travel more comfortably in and with life. Money is the tool in which I'll experience profoundly; profoundly experiencing, profoundly walking, profoundly growing.

* Be selective in investments of your energy. Practice selective investments of your energy & with whom and how you enguage yourself. Inputs / outputs in forging greater alignments of your own true journey, & conductionism of life energy.

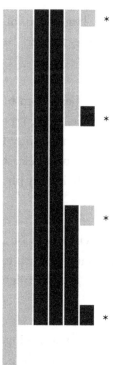

* Live artisticly rich and financial. Material richness & greater abundance, as this will allow you to work on being within your fuller potential, allowing you to be all that you can.

* In calling someone's / people's / another's bluff, by saying for example it's not the only financial game on the planet, you open yourself up to a multitude of business deals and financial opportunities.

* Materialise your plans through retaining your power, be strong and in your full power, making deals that suit you so as to be able to be free in going anywhere anytime.

* There is a profound abundance to the amount of people and deals available to you, the supply of synergistic life-giving forces to enaid you is infinite and there will always be more energy aligned towards you, now and in the future. Buy into the flow of abundance & prosperity.

* Apply one's effort consciously and constructively, eg - concerted action in the market place.

* Fund a quality that provides spiritual growth and allows you to build on your finances, assets and proprietary holdings, and artistic abilities.

* Financial richness unclutters my life. Rich is better for me, it frees me, propelling me into different and varied areas of growth where I can receive and give prolificly.

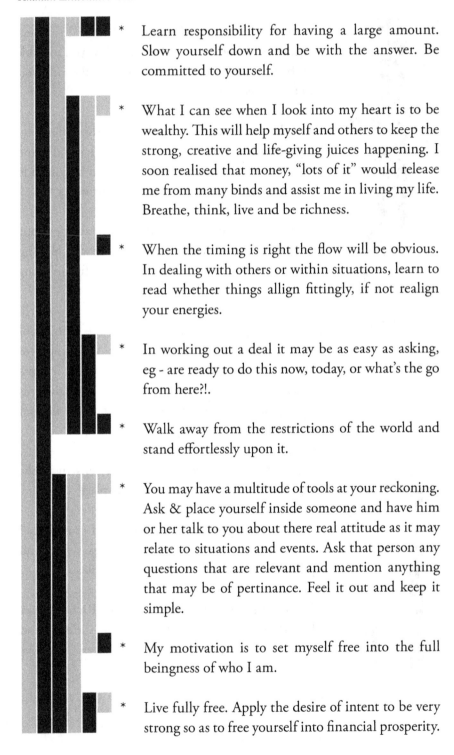

* Learn responsibility for having a large amount. Slow yourself down and be with the answer. Be committed to yourself.

* What I can see when I look into my heart is to be wealthy. This will help myself and others to keep the strong, creative and life-giving juices happening. I soon realised that money, "lots of it" would release me from many binds and assist me in living my life. Breathe, think, live and be richness.

* When the timing is right the flow will be obvious. In dealing with others or within situations, learn to read whether things allign fittingly, if not realign your energies.

* In working out a deal it may be as easy as asking, eg - are ready to do this now, today, or what's the go from here?!.

* Walk away from the restrictions of the world and stand effortlessly upon it.

* You may have a multitude of tools at your reckoning. Ask & place yourself inside someone and have him or her talk to you about there real attitude as it may relate to situations and events. Ask that person any questions that are relevant and mention anything that may be of pertinance. Feel it out and keep it simple.

* My motivation is to set myself free into the full beingness of who I am.

* Live fully free. Apply the desire of intent to be very strong so as to free yourself into financial prosperity.

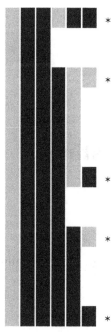

* Flow into an infinite perspective of reality and the world moving and changing to support me.

* When an uncompromised essence driveness takes charge an amazing flood of abundance takes place. Enjoy your own space, beingness & personal directionism.

* Travel light dear child of the universe, take baby steps as with those giant leaps occur.

* Oh my goodness, universe support and resonate with me. Enable me to create wealth in my life inwardly / outwardly & in my world in which I live.

* Charging properly to maximise financial wealth, time and energy expenditure and life arts is a vital key component to being abundantly wealthy. Affirm you will give value to yourself by charging what you're worth.

* Sometimes you have to be obvious when dealing with people.

PRAIR
(Lightness within manifesting one's desire)

* Prair - Pra = energy, Air = aether Prair, energy within the aether, even the smallest is felt...

* L.U.E. "Life the Universe and Everything".

* Holistic prair, eg's - please help universe. Let go, let god (god - being people, the all encompoassing god force, or the universal synergies that make this solid world that you inhabit & galaxy). Universe walk with me & help me in whatever I shall choose to do or be.

* Pray for the knowledge of what to pray for.

* Have faith but keep chipping away & make the moves that are going to support you it.

* Prair whatever one conceives or perceives prair to be "Good, Orderly, Direction etc".

* To put the footwork in but leave it within god's divine theatre. God's divine theatre being - (higher self / the powers that be "synergies".

* The universe helps those that help themselves, keep within the forward momentum of seeing providence made inwardly and outwardly manifest.

* Where would you like to see yourself in the future?!.

* What would you like in your life inwardly and outwardly?!.

* To ask but let go of the outcome, eg - what is it one desires most?, ie happiness, a feeling of lightness, contentment, security, financial wealth, abundance, variety, the richer juices of what life has to / on offer.

* Let go, let god. The universal child is the sort of person to trip over a bar of gold as you take life in your stride while living certifiable faith and lightness within living onesself seeing your dream reality made manifest, The universe is essentially steering you where you wish to steer yourself, learn to have your energies and focal powers refined into being a god / goddess creator of high potency.

* It may be but a whisper but say it. The power of articulation is wondrous in the healing and manifesting arts.

* Learn to articulate with fullness your desires & that which is for your own benefit.

* Prair is acknowleded, "inwardly and outwardly, subtle seed planting".

* What is it you want?, eg - do you want extra sensory perception?, super-powers,?, high levels of financial richness?, O.K. you got it!.

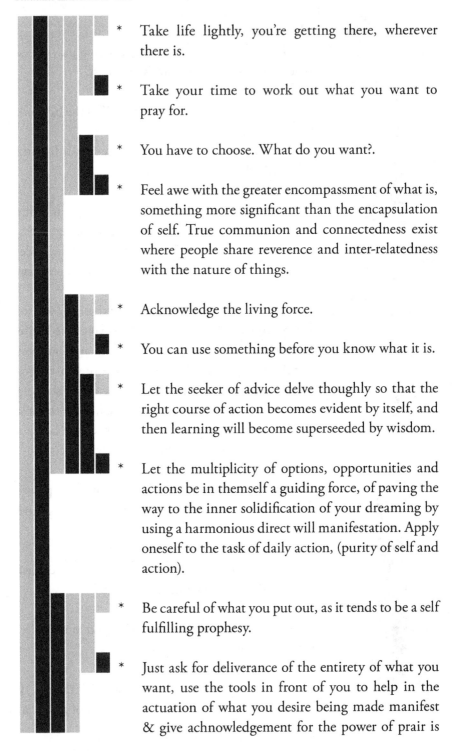

* Take life lightly, you're getting there, wherever there is.

* Take your time to work out what you want to pray for.

* You have to choose. What do you want?.

* Feel awe with the greater encompassment of what is, something more significant than the encapsulation of self. True communion and connectedness exist where people share reverence and inter-relatedness with the nature of things.

* Acknowledge the living force.

* You can use something before you know what it is.

* Let the seeker of advice delve thoughly so that the right course of action becomes evident by itself, and then learning will become superseeded by wisdom.

* Let the multiplicity of options, opportunities and actions be in themself a guiding force, of paving the way to the inner solidification of your dreaming by using a harmonious direct will manifestation. Apply oneself to the task of daily action, (purity of self and action).

* Be careful of what you put out, as it tends to be a self fulfilling prophesy.

* Just ask for deliverance of the entirety of what you want, use the tools in front of you to help in the actuation of what you desire being made manifest & give achnowledgement for the power of prair is

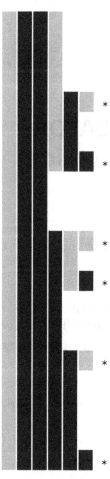

empowered that which you have put out for and received to date, as you continue to see manifest that which you desire for the future.

* Strength comes from subtle multiplicity with intricacy.

* Live and work with the god force of all that is within the solution, from your most holistic base & into the outside world around you.

* Prair is creating.

* Prair ~ Turning essence, to thought & now into action, to see manifest solidly within three dimensional reality.

* Prair ~ is a statement to the here & now, while being in the continued momentum & provodence of continued creation. Living now, moment to moment, instant to instant.

* Please feel light and positive!. How do I feel?. Why do I feel like this?. What could embetter this situation that I may find inwardly or outwardly etc.

GOD'S, DEITIES, GOD CREATOR
(Life, the universe and everything)

* Mu - empowerment of an object or thing. To put into solid form.

* Move away from the ritualistic type dogma, a projection out from self as the source (finiting the infinite). Based apon previous conditioning. Forge create & be anew.

* There is only one religion although there are many versions of it.

* You are entitled to a god of your own understanding. Eg's - The powers that be / the unfathomable / life, the universe and everything / let your god be one that looks after you & wants that which you want for yourself. You might not know presently what it is; it's good to stay true to being and what is real to you. Go about creating harmony & flow with words and the various parts of what is your own projected and reflected world that you find yourself in. Harmony and connectedness come when one is in harmony and connected. Try not to finite the infinite or get too dogmatic in one's present views and opinions, "it is what it is and you are what you are!".

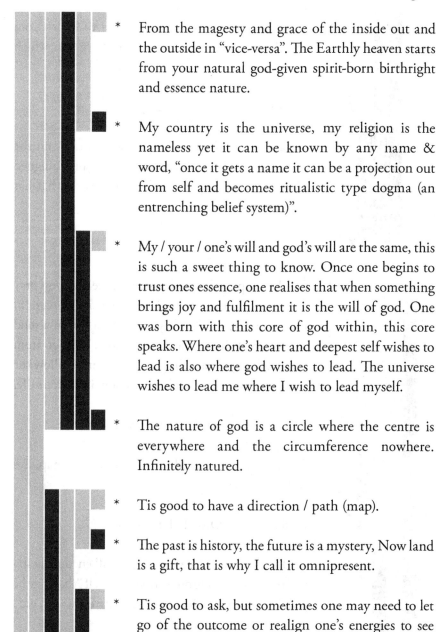

* From the magesty and grace of the inside out and the outside in "vice-versa". The Earthly heaven starts from your natural god-given spirit-born birthright and essence nature.

* My country is the universe, my religion is the nameless yet it can be known by any name & word, "once it gets a name it can be a projection out from self and becomes ritualistic type dogma (an entrenching belief system)".

* My / your / one's will and god's will are the same, this is such a sweet thing to know. Once one begins to trust ones essence, one realises that when something brings joy and fulfilment it is the will of god. One was born with this core of god within, this core speaks. Where one's heart and deepest self wishes to lead is also where god wishes to lead. The universe wishes to lead me where I wish to lead myself.

* The nature of god is a circle where the centre is everywhere and the circumference nowhere. Infinitely natured.

* Tis good to have a direction / path (map).

* The past is history, the future is a mystery, Now land is a gift, that is why I call it omnipresent.

* Tis good to ask, but sometimes one may need to let go of the outcome or realign one's energies to see your dreams fulfilled.

* God helps those that go about helping oneself.

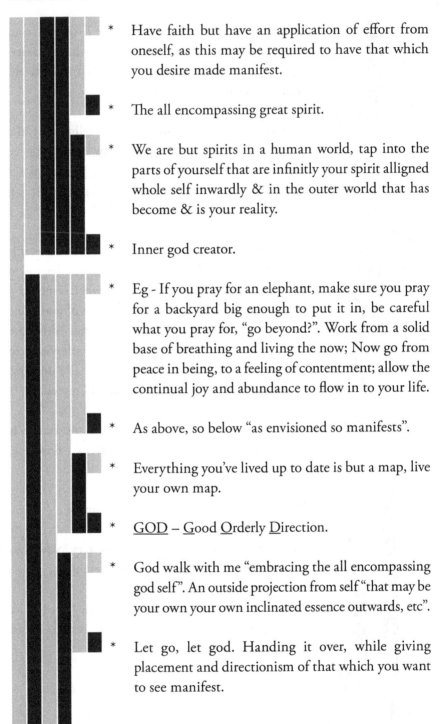

* Have faith but have an application of effort from oneself, as this may be required to have that which you desire made manifest.

* The all encompassing great spirit.

* We are but spirits in a human world, tap into the parts of yourself that are infinitly your spirit alligned whole self inwardly & in the outer world that has become & is your reality.

* Inner god creator.

* Eg - If you pray for an elephant, make sure you pray for a backyard big enough to put it in, be careful what you pray for, "go beyond?". Work from a solid base of breathing and living the now; Now go from peace in being, to a feeling of contentment; allow the continual joy and abundance to flow in to your life.

* As above, so below "as envisioned so manifests".

* Everything you've lived up to date is but a map, live your own map.

* <u>GOD</u> – <u>G</u>ood <u>O</u>rderly <u>D</u>irection.

* God walk with me "embracing the all encompassing god self". An outside projection from self "that may be your own your own inclinated essence outwards, etc".

* Let go, let god. Handing it over, while giving placement and directionism of that which you want to see manifest.

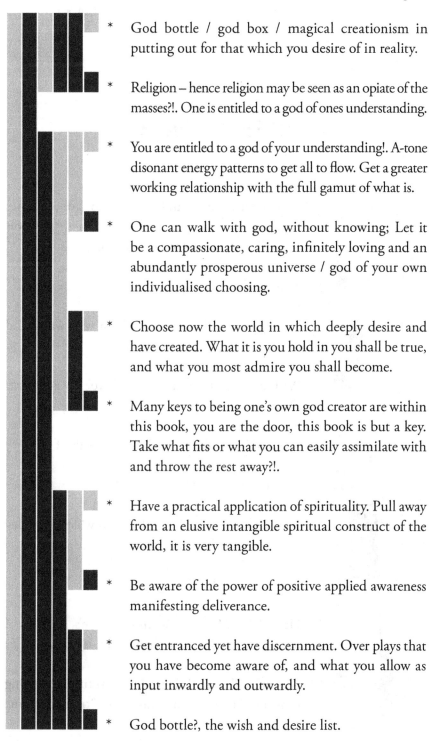

* God bottle / god box / magical creationism in putting out for that which you desire of in reality.

* Religion – hence religion may be seen as an opiate of the masses?!. One is entitled to a god of ones understanding.

* You are entitled to a god of your understanding!. A-tone disonant energy patterns to get all to flow. Get a greater working relationship with the full gamut of what is.

* One can walk with god, without knowing; Let it be a compassionate, caring, infinitely loving and an abundantly prosperous universe / god of your own individualised choosing.

* Choose now the world in which deeply desire and have created. What it is you hold in you shall be true, and what you most admire you shall become.

* Many keys to being one's own god creator are within this book, you are the door, this book is but a key. Take what fits or what you can easily assimilate with and throw the rest away?!.

* Have a practical application of spirituality. Pull away from an elusive intangible spiritual construct of the world, it is very tangible.

* Be aware of the power of positive applied awareness manifesting deliverance.

* Get entranced yet have discernment. Over plays that you have become aware of, and what you allow as input inwardly and outwardly.

* God bottle?, the wish and desire list.

TIME & SPACE

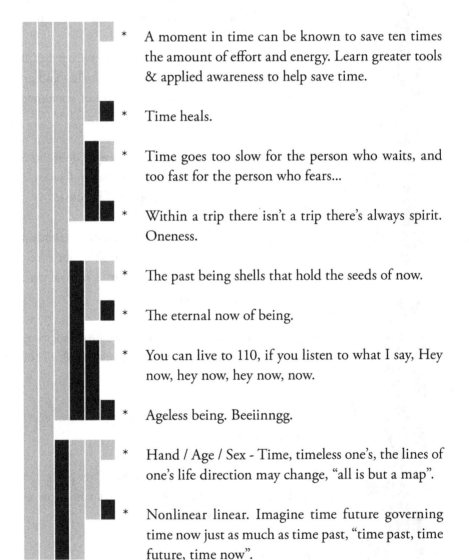

* A moment in time can be known to save ten times the amount of effort and energy. Learn greater tools & applied awareness to help save time.

* Time heals.

* Time goes too slow for the person who waits, and too fast for the person who fears...

* Within a trip there isn't a trip there's always spirit. Oneness.

* The past being shells that hold the seeds of now.

* The eternal now of being.

* You can live to 110, if you listen to what I say, Hey now, hey now, hey now, now.

* Ageless being. Beeiinngg.

* Hand / Age / Sex - Time, timeless one's, the lines of one's life direction may change, "all is but a map".

* Nonlinear linear. Imagine time future governing time now just as much as time past, "time past, time future, time now".

* Time conquers all.

* Time - when occupying two spaces at the same time, one occupies a no space, no time and an every space, everytime. Light may take time to travel, but one is forever receiving it in the now.

* Within, the key to everything is hidden within time. It may be hidden within "laying dormant awaiting to be found again", awaiting clarity, harmony and greater harmonic resolve. Keys — Within and without, tiz like having a two way mirror happening, the power of the objective observer and to look without judgement.

* Never ending story. I am balanced and have all the time in the world.

* Mayan archetype "only through time is time conquered".

* Window in the sky.

* Heaven on earth - ray of heaven - one can access the transmutable law of time by looking at the clouds, ie - one opens up to a space of beingness, eg - open up to the oneness, then while in that space bewithin the clouds till they become transfixed. It's the start of the process, and the conscious space required for some of the workings of "The Living Art", the ability of accessing the door to slowing down and being within all time, and all space, and being within the fullness that is all things.

* Time accommodates.

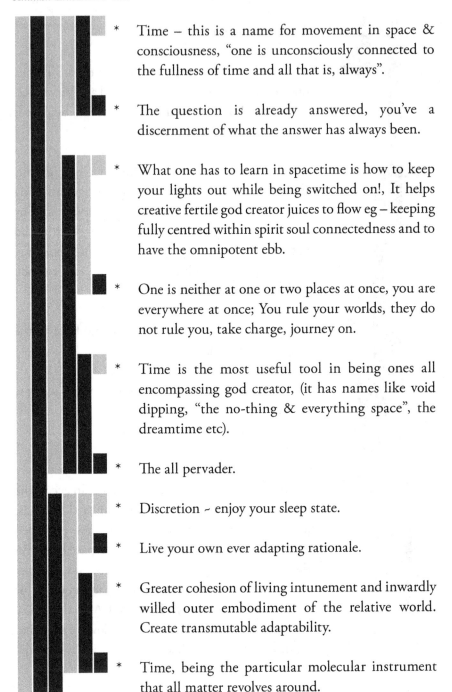

* Time – this is a name for movement in space & consciousness, "one is unconsciously connected to the fullness of time and all that is, always".

* The question is already answered, you've a discernment of what the answer has always been.

* What one has to learn in spacetime is how to keep your lights out while being switched on!, It helps creative fertile god creator juices to flow eg – keeping fully centred within spirit soul connectedness and to have the omnipotent ebb.

* One is neither at one or two places at once, you are everywhere at once; You rule your worlds, they do not rule you, take charge, journey on.

* Time is the most useful tool in being ones all encompassing god creator, (it has names like void dipping, "the no-thing & everything space", the dreamtime etc).

* The all pervader.

* Discretion ~ enjoy your sleep state.

* Live your own ever adapting rationale.

* Greater cohesion of living intunement and inwardly willed outer embodiment of the relative world. Create transmutable adaptability.

* Time, being the particular molecular instrument that all matter revolves around.

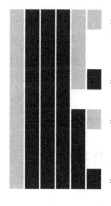

* We create time for ourselves, be careful of what you create for yourself.

* Time is a tool of accommodation.

* Time allows our consciousness to understand the journey that we are on. All will be revealed in time.

* Understand that we exist in a multitude of different and concurrent nows; like a vertical spike with different now's layered one over the other.

HOLISTIC
(Broad / all encompassing)

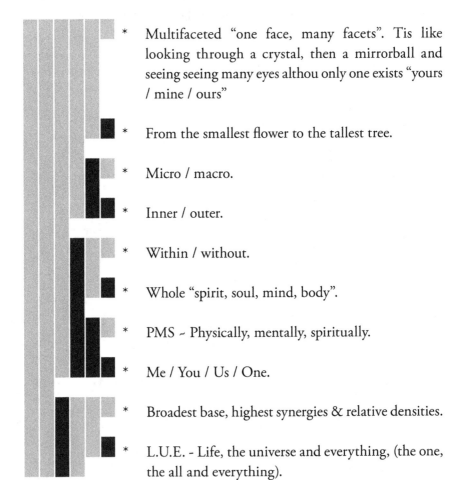

* Multifaceted "one face, many facets". Tis like looking through a crystal, then a mirrorball and seeing seeing many eyes althou only one exists "yours / mine / ours"

* From the smallest flower to the tallest tree.

* Micro / macro.

* Inner / outer.

* Within / without.

* Whole "spirit, soul, mind, body".

* PMS ~ Physically, mentally, spiritually.

* Me / You / Us / One.

* Broadest base, highest synergies & relative densities.

* L.U.E. - Life, the universe and everything, (the one, the all and everything).

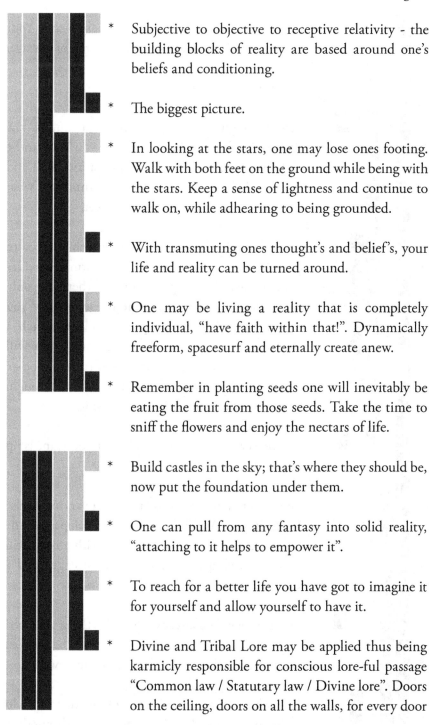

* Subjective to objective to receptive relativity - the building blocks of reality are based around one's beliefs and conditioning.

* The biggest picture.

* In looking at the stars, one may lose ones footing. Walk with both feet on the ground while being with the stars. Keep a sense of lightness and continue to walk on, while adhearing to being grounded.

* With transmuting ones thought's and belief's, your life and reality can be turned around.

* One may be living a reality that is completely individual, "have faith within that!". Dynamically freeform, spacesurf and eternally create anew.

* Remember in planting seeds one will inevitably be eating the fruit from those seeds. Take the time to sniff the flowers and enjoy the nectars of life.

* Build castles in the sky; that's where they should be, now put the foundation under them.

* One can pull from any fantasy into solid reality, "attaching to it helps to empower it".

* To reach for a better life you have got to imagine it for yourself and allow yourself to have it.

* Divine and Tribal Lore may be applied thus being karmicly responsible for conscious lore-ful passage "Common law / Statutary law / Divine lore". Doors on the ceiling, doors on all the walls, for every door there is a passage with its song for you to sing. Your true essence is the main song for any rite of passage.

* What matters most?!!!.

* Just through saying something it enters the probability for it to be. What is it you want to be and have around you as life and reality. Have and keep a solid base, one of healthy discernment of what you want. Your attachments empower.

* Everything is relative and very much subject to one's beliefs and conditioning, in nature there are neither rewards nor punishments, there are only consequences. The self manifestation of how you attach and what you empower. If you attach a construct of negatively slanted recourse you will more than likely receive such, it doesn't have to be so; attach positively and that's what will filter through. Choice's - the choice is in the choosing.

* The power to make the world what you want is up to you. Learn to direct will manifest.

* The power of manifesting, "totally or varying levels" is within you. As things become more apparent, the clarity to be able to see and deal with things will also come, clarity becomes a great strength and a valuable tool.

* Discernment, you already have everything you need to make the world what you want, use the tools in front of you. The need to live fresh and new.

* Individual leaf on the same tree of life, this will help endeavour the embrace of ones self with another,

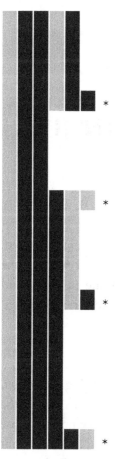

(one never looses self). Some others maybe on a simular branch to yourself, where-as some others maybe on the other side of the tree of life.

* To manifest totally or on varying levels. As things become more apparent, the clarity to be able to see and deal with it will also come. Clarity becomes a great strength and a valuable tool.

* Layered, from ones inner most core ie - from self, to consciousness, to breathing, to the senses and well being, to externals etc. Fine tune where you would like to see / find yourself. Linear.

* Where does one see oneself within the big picture?. Be comfortable with that and learn to have a self guidance system happening. Be at peace, work from the basics and have a strong foundation, something more comfortable and befitting like a houseboat cruising down the river of life.

* Life, externals, dimensions, the universe, any perception / conception / dream etc, is but a peg holding the boat to the endless sea, (it helps in the letting go, aiding one to embrace freedom, liberation and get one back on track from one's essence). Infinity

RELATIONSHIPS / PARTNER
(Male & Female)

* What is it to you?, All in this world you have created, you would not have liked this world without the features it has in it. There is value in being and walking within all of life's many and varied offerings!

* Like paths.

* Two wholes. Two people complementing each other, eg - one person may be good at maths, while the other may be good at english. It may not be a case of bringing the other person into that awareness, but maybe a case of acknowledging the other's assets, differences, and the life energy you receive. Being and sharing your journey together.

* Connection / Interconnection / Communication.

* Resonance / Atonement / Lightness.

* At-one-meant / In-to-me-see. The ability to look, and be fully with another, while having respect for the other, and respect in regards to inner and outer spaces.

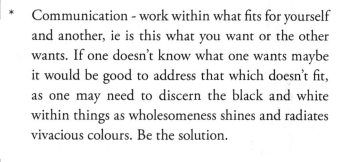

* Communication - work within what fits for yourself and another, ie is this what you want or the other wants. If one doesn't know what one wants maybe it would be good to address that which doesn't fit, as one may need to discern the black and white within things as wholesomeness shines and radiates vivacious colours. Be the solution.

* Giving of the life and pure love energy, thinking of yourself as the other.

* Better to have gained through experience and have given of your loving life energy. If parting comes, let it be a parting, not serving as a severance in the present now land and the day to day living of your dream life. Thank life for the experience and know that there is richer more profound experiences to be had as the best is yet to come always.

* If you want something set it free, while living within truth, purity, who and where you're currently at. If it's meant to be, there may be a lot more to be gained through being / sharing / adventuring / living together.

* Non-clingy / possessiveness.

* To look in and out together. Look for the similarities within sharing and being with another both inwardly and outwardly.

* Complementing each other, "someone of parring, two strong individuals, giving of the life energy, filling each other's vessel", living life in richness selflessly.

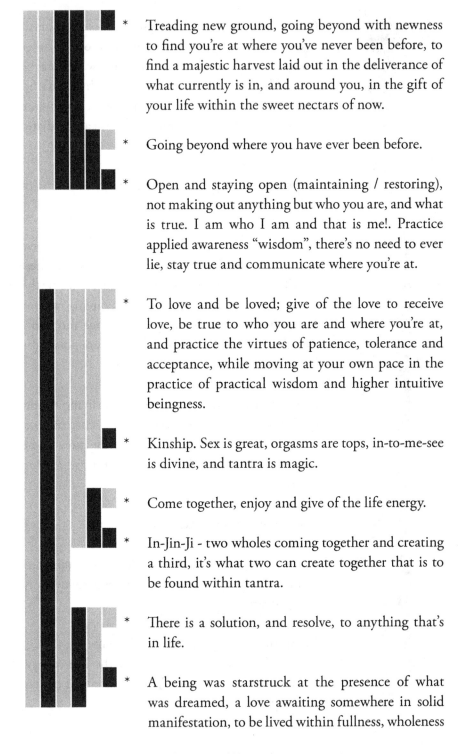

* Treading new ground, going beyond with newness to find you're at where you've never been before, to find a majestic harvest laid out in the deliverance of what currently is in, and around you, in the gift of your life within the sweet nectars of now.

* Going beyond where you have ever been before.

* Open and staying open (maintaining / restoring), not making out anything but who you are, and what is true. I am who I am and that is me!. Practice applied awareness "wisdom", there's no need to ever lie, stay true and communicate where you're at.

* To love and be loved; give of the love to receive love, be true to who you are and where you're at, and practice the virtues of patience, tolerance and acceptance, while moving at your own pace in the practice of practical wisdom and higher intuitive beingness.

* Kinship. Sex is great, orgasms are tops, in-to-me-see is divine, and tantra is magic.

* Come together, enjoy and give of the life energy.

* In-Jin-Ji - two wholes coming together and creating a third, it's what two can create together that is to be found within tantra.

* There is a solution, and resolve, to anything that's in life.

* A being was starstruck at the presence of what was dreamed, a love awaiting somewhere in solid manifestation, to be lived within fullness, wholeness

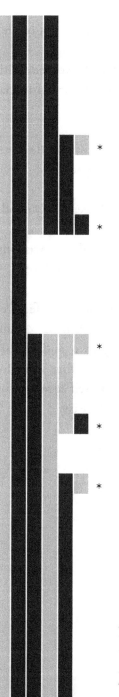

and enrapturement, of the togetherness of the love for life as the magic, providence and synchronicity bring in the elixirs of the universal bounty, ie – as if being kissed and advocated by the most supreme. Relax and be, enjoy, yummee.

* Love the twists and turns, and all of one's traits. Learn to readapt to who you are and be and forge anew.

* Darkness is the absence of light, from which all things come, when light has the absence of darkness and both live in happy communion, at each moment I have the power to transform my world by what I have learned.

* Thank the past; constructively review it and plant new seeds as there's much to be gained in the way of unexpected fresh new life experiences to come.

* To have and to hold, (The conscious living embodiment of one's chosen fullness).

* The Wedding. Be it of and in fullness, in some way, manner, shape or form, so as to be and enaid symbiotic union. Create your own vows, and get it so it works. Does it resonate for you as an individual, in the other, and in togetherness?!. The vows of consecration - to create atonement the vows can be made up "adapted" to be mutually fitting for you and the other. Two individuals committing to each other wholly, while living a unified front of a karmic journey of oneness, togetherness & fullness. There is much to be had in being true to being and communicating your fuller truth.

* Enjoyment of the journey. Get the most out of life.

* The manner and validity in which we deal with things can be seen as a measure of our existential size.

* Preserve the sanctity of self, the union of togetherness, and the bestowment of past deliverances.

* Constructively review the past. Be genuinely good.

* Peace. It can be attributed to excellence, wisdom, refinement and is a talent of many a great love.

* One can create one's own commitments, & feel free to change them; they can be recommitted & built upon. Old spaces may be outgrown and require readaption. Create working inroads that work for you, and the other. In giving to yourself & respecting the vestige of who you are. Breathe easy.

LOVE

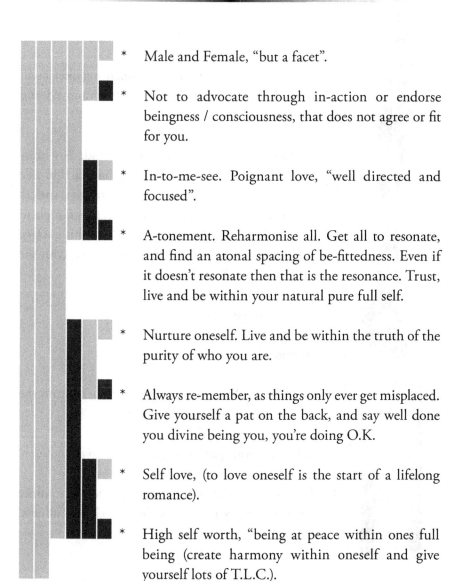

* Male and Female, "but a facet".

* Not to advocate through in-action or endorse beingness / consciousness, that does not agree or fit for you.

* In-to-me-see. Poignant love, "well directed and focused".

* A-tonement. Reharmonise all. Get all to resonate, and find an atonal spacing of be-fittedness. Even if it doesn't resonate then that is the resonance. Trust, live and be within your natural pure full self.

* Nurture oneself. Live and be within the truth of the purity of who you are.

* Always re-member, as things only ever get misplaced. Give yourself a pat on the back, and say well done you divine being you, you're doing O.K.

* Self love, (to love oneself is the start of a lifelong romance).

* High self worth, "being at peace within ones full being (create harmony within oneself and give yourself lots of T.L.C.).

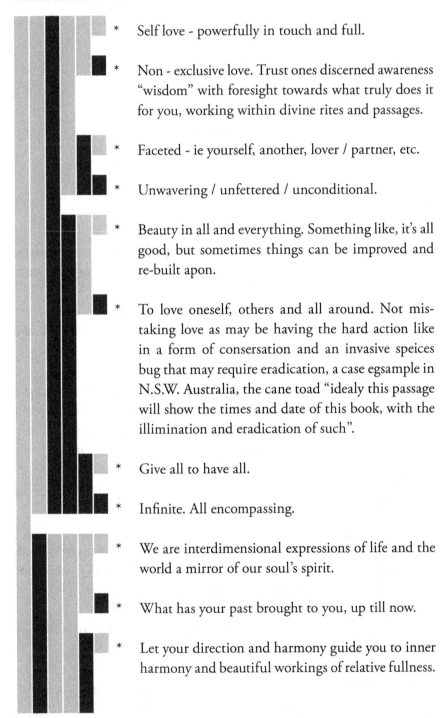

* Self love - powerfully in touch and full.

* Non - exclusive love. Trust ones discerned awareness "wisdom" with foresight towards what truly does it for you, working within divine rites and passages.

* Faceted - ie yourself, another, lover / partner, etc.

* Unwavering / unfettered / unconditional.

* Beauty in all and everything. Something like, it's all good, but sometimes things can be improved and re-built apon.

* To love oneself, others and all around. Not mistaking love as may be having the hard action like in a form of consersation and an invasive speices bug that may require eradication, a case egsample in N.S.W. Australia, the cane toad "idealy this passage will show the times and date of this book, with the illimination and eradication of such".

* Give all to have all.

* Infinite. All encompassing.

* We are interdimensional expressions of life and the world a mirror of our soul's spirit.

* What has your past brought to you, up till now.

* Let your direction and harmony guide you to inner harmony and beautiful workings of relative fullness.

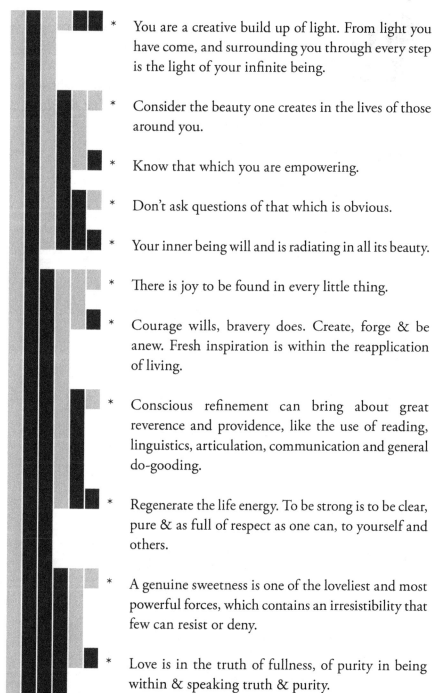

* You are a creative build up of light. From light you have come, and surrounding you through every step is the light of your infinite being.

* Consider the beauty one creates in the lives of those around you.

* Know that which you are empowering.

* Don't ask questions of that which is obvious.

* Your inner being will and is radiating in all its beauty.

* There is joy to be found in every little thing.

* Courage wills, bravery does. Create, forge & be anew. Fresh inspiration is within the reapplication of living.

* Conscious refinement can bring about great reverence and providence, like the use of reading, linguistics, articulation, communication and general do-gooding.

* Regenerate the life energy. To be strong is to be clear, pure & as full of respect as one can, to yourself and others.

* A genuine sweetness is one of the loveliest and most powerful forces, which contains an irresistibility that few can resist or deny.

* Love is in the truth of fullness, of purity in being within & speaking truth & purity.

* Shining greater love and light into the impression of our now which is always in flux.

* Shining / Shine greater love into the light of our "your / my" now, which is always but the shells of our past, giving way for newness.

CHI, ENERGY, OM

* Chi ~ universal life force.

* Reiki ~ Rei "soul / spirit", Ki "universal energy"; One's soul / spirit alignment and intunement with universal energy.

* There is much life energy to be had within a state of positive, constructive & life giving energy to yourself and to all others. The attributes be but virtue itself.

* Inner peace, "One is omnipotent when tapped into a state where one is at peace".

* Breathing.

* Refined synergy, "energy from life giving food".

* Life energy, "that which is nurturing and sustaining to ones being".

* Resonance, "being able to resonate with all things (no static energy)".

* Prair, "pra-air, energy within the aether, even the smallest is felt".

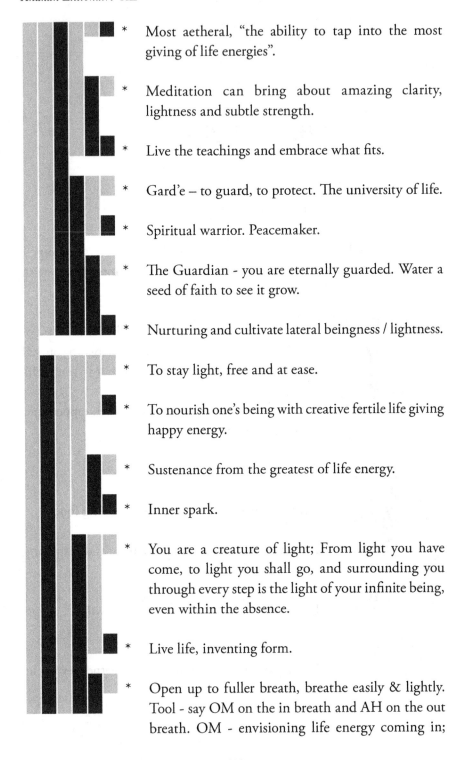

* Most aetheral, "the ability to tap into the most giving of life energies".

* Meditation can bring about amazing clarity, lightness and subtle strength.

* Live the teachings and embrace what fits.

* Gard'e – to guard, to protect. The university of life.

* Spiritual warrior. Peacemaker.

* The Guardian - you are eternally guarded. Water a seed of faith to see it grow.

* Nurturing and cultivate lateral beingness / lightness.

* To stay light, free and at ease.

* To nourish one's being with creative fertile life giving happy energy.

* Sustenance from the greatest of life energy.

* Inner spark.

* You are a creature of light; From light you have come, to light you shall go, and surrounding you through every step is the light of your infinite being, even within the absence.

* Live life, inventing form.

* Open up to fuller breath, breathe easily & lightly. Tool - say OM on the in breath and AH on the out breath. OM - envisioning life energy coming in;

and AH - feeling and allowing the release of energy on the out, and vortexed into a black hole to be resynthesised into the universal life energy of the greater good within all that is.

* Relax keep energies contained, "the release of form is a good way (dynamically flowing)". There is many a tool one can use as required, ie - different focal tools of empowerment.

* Clear level eyes.

* Find lightness in everything. Illumination, create brighter focus.

* The living force, is in flow always; "If it is not there, it is not in the known conceived universe of the infinite probabilities of you. LIVE THE LIVING FORCE.

* The different possibilities of paradox; can disprove or prove anything, so your only running your own race / space. Its good to swim the sea but come to shore and see what you would like to create for yourself; to have and to hold.

* In freeing oneself up one can convert from a low resonance person, to one of high resonance.

* What you are attracts!.

* Learn to taste what you consume, in all ways.

* Be careful what your feeding out and into, "personal refinement of choosing, it's like a mirror you get to see through".

FREEDOM

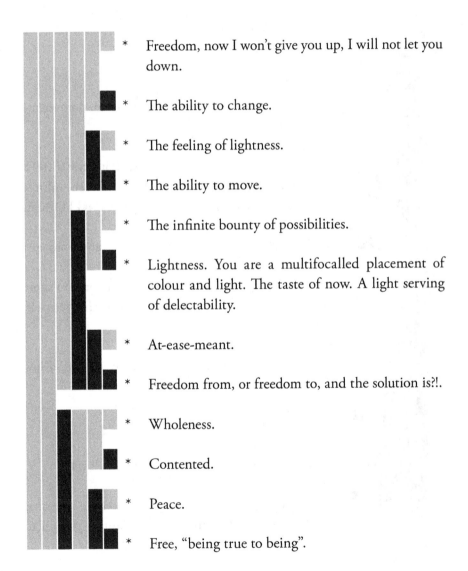

* Freedom, now I won't give you up, I will not let you down.

* The ability to change.

* The feeling of lightness.

* The ability to move.

* The infinite bounty of possibilities.

* Lightness. You are a multifocalled placement of colour and light. The taste of now. A light serving of delectability.

* At-ease-meant.

* Freedom from, or freedom to, and the solution is?!.

* Wholeness.

* Contented.

* Peace.

* Free, "being true to being".

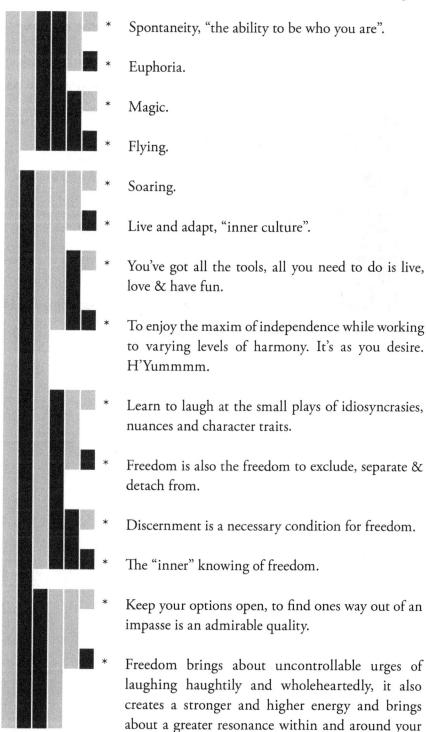

* Spontaneity, "the ability to be who you are".

* Euphoria.

* Magic.

* Flying.

* Soaring.

* Live and adapt, "inner culture".

* You've got all the tools, all you need to do is live, love & have fun.

* To enjoy the maxim of independence while working to varying levels of harmony. It's as you desire. H'Yummmm.

* Learn to laugh at the small plays of idiosyncrasies, nuances and character traits.

* Freedom is also the freedom to exclude, separate & detach from.

* Discernment is a necessary condition for freedom.

* The "inner" knowing of freedom.

* Keep your options open, to find ones way out of an impasse is an admirable quality.

* Freedom brings about uncontrollable urges of laughing haughtily and wholeheartedly, it also creates a stronger and higher energy and brings about a greater resonance within and around your

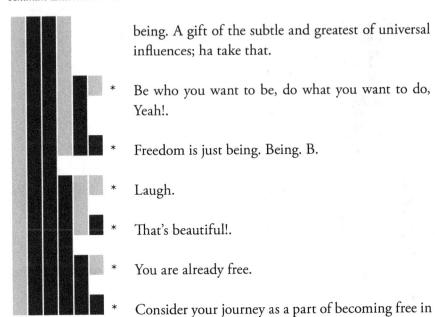

being. A gift of the subtle and greatest of universal influences; ha take that.

*   Be who you want to be, do what you want to do, Yeah!.

*   Freedom is just being. Being. B.

*   Laugh.

*   That's beautiful!.

*   You are already free.

*   Consider your journey as a part of becoming free in your reality, now what would that be?.

SPONTANEOUS

* Inner exuberance.

* Freedom in every moment.

* Just the way it is.

* Zip Zap Zippi Yi Yea Ha Yea, Zump pudy do da, zump puddy ay, my oh my vot a vunderful day.

* Do it, live it, be it.

* I will, to will thy will.

* Chew it up, consume, and process it.

* To be all one can be.

* Be as big as one can.

* Feel free to be whoever or whatever you are at any given time.

* Living life fully free.

* In living and being all you can, you help to empower others to do the same.

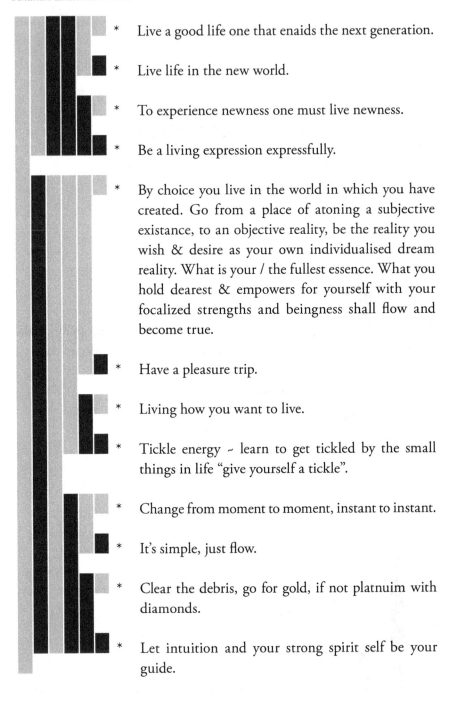

* Live a good life one that enaids the next generation.

* Live life in the new world.

* To experience newness one must live newness.

* Be a living expression expressfully.

* By choice you live in the world in which you have created. Go from a place of atoning a subjective existance, to an objective reality, be the reality you wish & desire as your own individualised dream reality. What is your / the fullest essence. What you hold dearest & empowers for yourself with your focalized strengths and beingness shall flow and become true.

* Have a pleasure trip.

* Living how you want to live.

* Tickle energy ~ learn to get tickled by the small things in life "give yourself a tickle".

* Change from moment to moment, instant to instant.

* It's simple, just flow.

* Clear the debris, go for gold, if not platnuim with diamonds.

* Let intuition and your strong spirit self be your guide.

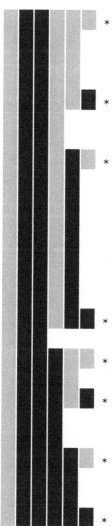

* Speak as though others were intelligent and that they know and understand. Human adaption to form is very impressive. Test the water then go for a swim.

* What do you want to do or what do you want to be in order to be free in this moment.

* All I ask is that you keep coming back to your essence and truest self!. Please keep in contact with the god force that is all things. I would and I believe others would greatly benefit from a relationship, with your higher fuller self as it would relate and operate within unionism with others and the world, "universal dreaming".

* Brain storming, "keep ones being a flowing".

* Constantly readapting.

* Elegance arises when the effort it took to achieve it has become invisible.

* Start of adventure, end of adventure, new adventure, adventure on.

* Enjoy the areas of the art of play, areas that are free of specific aims, be goal directed. That which is given to pure enjoyment, to dreaming and the feeling of creativity in dynamic flow within movement.

JOY

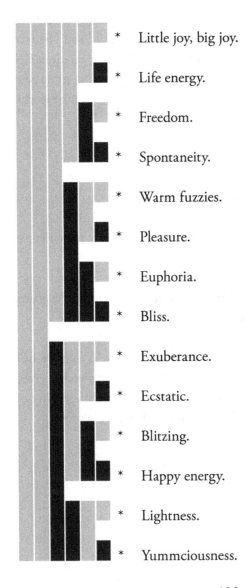

* Little joy, big joy.

* Life energy.

* Freedom.

* Spontaneity.

* Warm fuzzies.

* Pleasure.

* Euphoria.

* Bliss.

* Exuberance.

* Ecstatic.

* Blitzing.

* Happy energy.

* Lightness.

* Yummciousness.

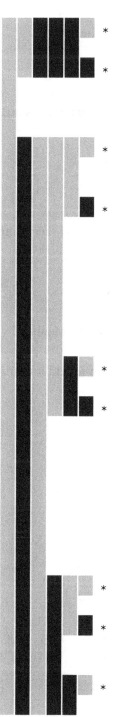

* Delicious.

* Joy is a precious gift, but it is for ourselves alone, we may share it with others. It radiates a magnetic attraction, energeticly life giving and soul warming.

* Command an even temper, a ready smile, a benevolent disposition and cheerful manner.

* Joie-de-vivre ~ People who have this are irresistible, no matter what one loves them, they are immensely attractive to the opposite sex and nothing gets them down for long. They are never bored and always have the feeling, the conviction that they are lucky; that happiness is the normal state of being and that they are indeed god's favourite children.

* Joy, Joy, Joy, the abundance of joy!.

* Enjoy your advancement and personal fulfilment, every step is a step forward, there is always positive to be found in everything. Create movement with your impasses, imagine you are in a tunnel crawling forwards; It's totally O.K. to stay where you are. You are never going back, and if there might be a block in the way. Envision yourself fluid, & eithericly pass through.

* Satisfaction is the reward of joy.

* Be within the self representation of "putting ones best foot forward".

* Being light free and happy is highly praised and attracts many a smiling happy compliance.

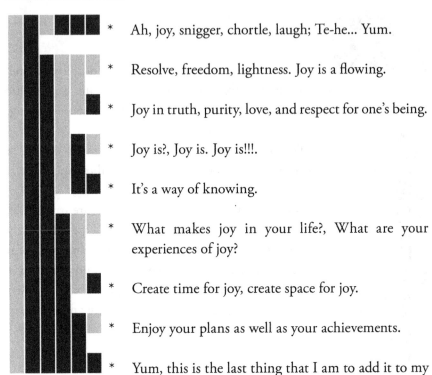

* Ah, joy, snigger, chortle, laugh; Te-he... Yum.

* Resolve, freedom, lightness. Joy is a flowing.

* Joy in truth, purity, love, and respect for one's being.

* Joy is?, Joy is. Joy is!!!.

* It's a way of knowing.

* What makes joy in your life?, What are your experiences of joy?

* Create time for joy, create space for joy.

* Enjoy your plans as well as your achievements.

* Yum, this is the last thing that I am to add it to my particular now land.

HEAVEN ON EARTH

* Relative to one's journey, ie - what is the dream reality.

* A reality of one's choosing "deepest desire", inwardly and outwardly.

* Extended homeland being the universe, "all encompassing heaven on earth".

* The ability to turn reality to one's choosing.

* Sniffing the roses - taking the time out to enjoy the smaller things in life, (with the small things comes great life energy).

* Universal reality, "the biggest picture (it is what it is / anything perceivable is possible, etc)". Relative reality, "the building blocks (What one attaches or sets up as belief)". One will find with any universal reality that a relative reality will form and become manifest to support it, it may not happen in one event or over night but it does and will happen, eventually.

* Do you wish to create friends of the same nature?, "one has to work it out for oneself". Gravitate towards

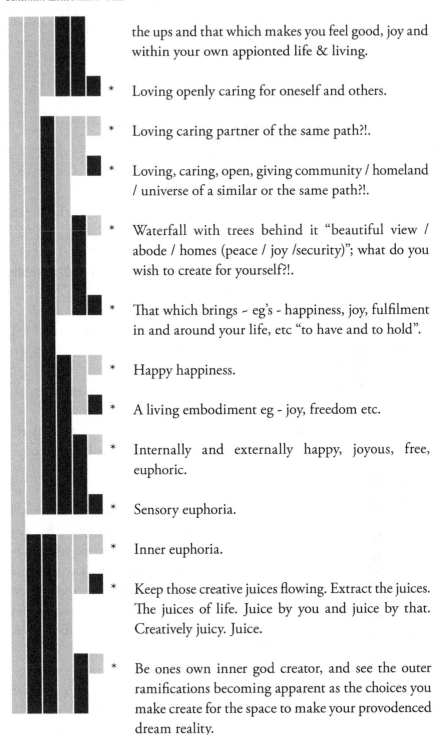

the ups and that which makes you feel good, joy and within your own appionted life & living.

* Loving openly caring for oneself and others.

* Loving caring partner of the same path?!.

* Loving, caring, open, giving community / homeland / universe of a similar or the same path?!.

* Waterfall with trees behind it "beautiful view / abode / homes (peace / joy /security)"; what do you wish to create for yourself?!.

* That which brings ~ eg's - happiness, joy, fulfilment in and around your life, etc "to have and to hold".

* Happy happiness.

* A living embodiment eg - joy, freedom etc.

* Internally and externally happy, joyous, free, euphoric.

* Sensory euphoria.

* Inner euphoria.

* Keep those creative juices flowing. Extract the juices. The juices of life. Juice by you and juice by that. Creatively juicy. Juice.

* Be ones own inner god creator, and see the outer ramifications becoming apparent as the choices you make create for the space to make your provodenced dream reality.

* A world of ones choosing. A universe of ones desired outcome in and around one.

* Divineness of everything. Syncronicity.

* Divine scenario.

* Choose your reality.

* Ambitions satisfied.

* Rewards received.

* Inner fondness. Lovely. XO

* Strong worldly messages, "divine truth resonance".

* The gifts of the universe are there, only you can discern what you want that to be.

* Ones dreams may change, grow, evolve and adapt, live the dream as whatever it is.

* I can change my direct reality now.

* I am walking my dream reality now.

* To achieve and have one's dream reality, all you have to do is live it, be it and do whatever it takes. Enjoy the process of the mutable law of ever unfolding infinite reality. That means now, live it beautiful. H'Yummmmmideee...

LIVE THE PERFECT DREAM LIFE LIVING!

Printed in the United States
By Bookmasters